ZOOM
in on
NATURE

Camilla de la Bédoyère

QED Publishing

Editor: Amanda Askew
Designer: Andrew Crowson
Picture Researcher: Maria Joannou

Copyright © QED Publishing 2011

First published in the UK in 2011 by
QED Publishing
A Quarto Group company
230 City Road
London EC1V 2TT

www.qed-publishing.co.uk

A catalogue record for this book is available from the British Library.

ISBN 978 1 84835 803 4

Printed in China

◀ Front cover: This is a
Southern Hawker dragonfly.
It has eyes on the side of
its head. They are called
compound eyes, which means
they are made up of thousands
of tiny parts.

Picture credits
Alamy Images Florian Franke 86t;
Corbis Micro Discovery 39tl, Tim Pannell 60t, Carole Valkenier/All Canada Photos 65tr, Stephen Frink/Science Faction 69tr, Dr. John D. Cunningham/Visuals Unlimited 93b, Fadil 97tr, Dennis Kunkel Microscopy, Inc./Visuals Unlimited 98b;
DK Images 23r, 36;
Flickr 86;
FLPA Front cover: Imagebroker, Mark Moffett/Minden Pictures 10b, Rolf Nussbaumer/Imagebroker 11bl, Thomas Marent/Minden Pictures 14b, Cisca Castelijns/FN/Minden Pictures 15cr, Mark Moffett/Minden Pictures 16b, Piotr Naskrecki/Minden Pictures 17b (background), Mark Moffett/Minden Pictures 18b, Murray Cooper/Minden Pictures 19b, Ingo Arndt 16b, Chien Lee/Minden Pictures 20t, Murray Cooper/Minden Pictures 21tl, Ingo Arndt 22b, Frans Lanting 23b, Michael Durham/Minden Pictures 24t, Mark Moffett/Minden Pictures 25b, Steve Trewhella 25cr, Albert Lleal/Minden Pictures 25tl, John Eveson 26-27t, Heidi & Hans-Juergen Koch/Minden Pictures 26br, Mark Moffett/Minden Pictures 27b, Gary K Smith 27t, James Christensen/Minden Pictures 28b, Albert Mans/FN/Minden 28t, Gerry Ellis/Minden Pictures 30-31, David Hosking 31bl, Mark Moffett/Minden Pictures 32cl, John Eveson 32br, Albert Mans/FN/Minden 33cl, Albert Lleal/Minden Pictures 33tl, Harri Taavetti 36b, 36-37t, Gerry Ellis/Minden Pictures 38b, Donald M. Jones 39tr, Photo Researchers 40c, Gerry Ellis/Minden Pictures 40b, John Hawkins 45b, Ingo Schulz/Imagebroker 49b, Wayne Hutchinson 51t, Frans Lanting 51b, John Zimmermann 52l, Jim Brandenburg/Minden Pictures 52r, Jurgen & Christine Sohns 52-53, Michael & Patricia Fogden/Minden Pictures 53tr, Frans Lanting 53b, S & D & K Maslowski 55bl, Richard Costin 57tr, Jurgen & Christine Sohns 58br, Harri Taavetti 58cl, Ingo Schulz/Imagebroker 59cl, Hiroya Minakuchi/Minden Pictures 62-63, Ingo Arndt/Minden Pictures 63bl, Konrad Wothe/Minden Pictures 64l, Fred Bavendam/Minden Pictures 66-67, Chris Newbert/Minden Pictures 67l, Fred Bavendam/Minden Pictures 67b, Silvestris Fotoservice 73b, Chris Newbert/Minden Pictures 75t, Imagebroker 78bl, Hiroya Minakuchi/Minden Pictures 79b, Norbert Wu/Minden Pictures 83bl, D P Wilson 89bl, Nigel Cattlin 97b, Sunset 99tl, Albert Lleal/Minden Pictures 99tr, Nigel Cattlin 101t, Thomas Marent/Minden Pictures 102b, Michael Dietrich/Imagebroker 103b, 105b, Justus de Cuveland/Imagebroker 106b, Mark Moffett/Minden Pictures 107b, Justus de Cuveland/Imagebroker 108b, Jan Vermeer/FN/Minden 108-109, Albert Lleal/Minden Pictures 110cr, Mark Moffett/Minden Pictures 111tl, Thomas Marent/Minden Pictures 111tr;
Getty Images 87;
Nature Picture Library Nature Production 5t, Stephen Dalton 12b(2), Doug Wechsler 21b, Nature Production 25tr, Meul/ARCO 26bl, Nick Upton 29br, 31br, Stephen Dalton 31t, Doug Wechsler 33cr, NPL 34-35, Jane Burton 34b, Philippe Clement 35b, Pete Cairns 37tr, Philippe Clement 37br, Charlie Hamilton James 39b, Rolf Nussbaumer 40-41t, Mike Potts 41tr, Wegner/ARCO 45tr, Wild Wonders of Europe/Varesvu 47tr, Wild Wonders of Europe/Widstrand 47b, Jane Burton 50b (stage 2), 51cl, Pete Cairns 54l, Andy Rouse 57b, Charlie Hamilton James 58t, Wild Wonders of Europe/Widstrand 58bl, Rolf Nussbaumer 59tr, Jane Burton 59cr, Andy Rouse 59bl, NPL 60-61, Rolf Nussbaumer 60, Steve Knell 62, Jose B. Ruiz 65c, Mark Carwardine 70b, Jurgen Freund 74b, Georgette Douwma 77c, Jane Burton 78-79, David Shale 80t, 82b, 82-83, 83br, Kim Taylor 88b, 88-89t, Duncan McEwan 92-93, Ross Hoddinott 94b, 96b, Thomas Lazar 103cl, Alex Hyde 103cr, Brian Lightfoot 104bl, Nick Gordon 107tl;
Photolibrary Flirt Collection/LWA-Dann Tardif 8t, Eastphoto Eastphoto 13tl, Age Fotostock 16t, Emanuele Biggi 17tl, Antonio Lopez Roman 18c, Last Refuge 24b, Martin Ruegner 29bl, Otto Hahn 29t, Age Fotostock 32bl, Otto Hahn 33bl, Oxford Scientific/Lewis Phillips 37bl, Phototake Science 42b, Juniors Bildarchiv 44c, Phototake Science 44b, Doug Allan 54b, Tony Tilford 55t, Doug Allan 56b, Tony Tilford 59br, Animals Animals/Joyce & Frank Burek 60t, Mirko Zanni 67c, Peter Arnold Images/Jonathan Bird 72l, Peter Arnold Images/Kelvin Aitken 75b, Oxford Scientific/Paulo de Oliveira 81t, Index Stock Imagery/Henryk T. Kaiser 86b, Index Stock Imagery 100bl, Index Stock Imagery/Henryk T. Kaiser 100-101, H Stanley Johnson 104-105, 110br, Index Stock Imagery/Henryk T. Kaiser 111bl;

Photoshot NHPA/Mark Bowler 11t, NHPA/Stephen Dalton 17b, 21tr, NHPA/Nick Garbutt 41b, NHPA/M I Walker 89tr, NHPA/A.N.T. Photo Library 105t, NHPA/Laurie Campbell 108c;
Science Photo Library Tom McHugh 8b, Richard R Hansen 9b, 11br, Claude Nuridsany & Marie Perennou 12b(1), 12b(3), 12b(4), Tom McHugh 17tr, Eye of Science 22t, Tom McHugh 32cr, Steve Gschmeissner 43tl, Herve Conge, ISM 50b (stage 1), Kenneth H Thomas 51cr, Steve Gschmeissner 62b, Wim Van Egmond/Visuals Unlimited 63tr, M.I. Walker 63br, Alexander Semenov 64r, Steve Gschmeissner 65tl, Eye of Science 68t, Science Pictures Ltd 69tl, Dr. Hossler/Visuals Unlimited 69b, M.H. Sharp 70t, Alexis Rosenfeld 71b, Alexander Semenov 73tl, Kjell B.Sandved 73tr, Matthew Oldfield 74c, Peter Scoones 76t, Power and Syred 76b, Matthew Oldfield 77t, Gustav Verderber/Visuals Unlimited 78br, Wim Van Egmond/Visuals Unlimited 79t, David Wrobel/Visuals Unlimited 80b, Dr Ken MacDonald 81bl, Sinclair Stammers 83t, Power and Syred 84bl, Alexander Semenov 84br, 85tl, Jan Hinsch 87b, 7br, David Nunuk 90t, Eye of Science 90b, Dr Keith Wheeler 91tl, Steve Gschmeissner 91tr, Claude Nuridsany & Marie Perennou 91b, Eye of Science 92b, Susumu Nishinaga 93t, Adrian Thomas 94l, Merlin Tuttle 106t, Art Wolfe 107tr, Eye of Science 109b, Jan Hinsch 110t, Steve Gschmeissner 111cr, Adrian Thomas 112; **Shutterstock** Matthew Cole 8-9, Karbunar 10-11, Studiotouch 12t, Pan Xunbin 13b, Eric Isselée 13cr, Dr. Morley Read 13tr, Chas 14-15, Pan Xunbin 15b, Alslutsky 15t, Liew Weng Keong 18-19t, Dr. Morley Read 19tr, Tischenko Irina 22-21, Matthew Cole 30b, Tischenko Irina 32t, Chas 33br, Eric Isselée 33tr, Blacqbook 34t, Frog-traveller 35t, Iv Nikolny 38t, Chris Pole 42l, MustafaNC 43tr, Nicholas Moore 43b, Joanne Harris and Daniel Bubnich 44-45, Eduardo Rivero 46l, Bernd Schmidt 46b, Dhoxax 47tl, Christian Musat 48c, Bernd Schmidt 48b, Stephen Chung 48-49, Frog-traveller 49t, Valentina_G 50t, Saied Shahin Kiya 50b (stage 3), Xavier Marchant 55br, Chris Alcock 56t, Martin Pateman 56-57, Iv Nikolny 58cr, Eduardo Rivero 59tl, Teguh Tirtaputra 60b, Cigdem Sean Cooper 70-71, Johan1900 71tr, Basel101658 92cl, Mary Lane 95tl, R McKown 95tr, Maslov Dmitry 95b, Nito 96c, Wong Hock Weng 96-97, Joseph Scott Photography 98t, Tatiana Makotra 99b, Newa 100br, Tatiana Makotra 101b, EuToch 102t, Thien Eu 103t, Calvin Chan 104br, Evlakhov Valeriy 109tr, EuToch 110bl, R McKown 110cl, Calvin Chan 111cl, Wong Hock Weng 111br, Matthew Cole 116; Loskutnikov 119.

Words in **bold** can be found in the Glossary
on pages 112–114.

CONTENTS

ZOOM INTO...   6

BUGS

READY FOR ACTION   10

GROWING UP   12

BIG-EYED BUGS   14

JAWS AND CLAWS   16

ANTS UNITED   18

HIDDEN FROM VIEW   20

BEAUTIFUL BUGS   22

ON THE MOVE   24

HONEY MONSTERS   26

SPOTS AND STRIPES   28

HAIRY NOT SCARY   30

USE YOUR EYES   32

BIRDS

SILENT BUT DEADLY   36

HIGH FLIERS   38

SPEEDY WINGS   40

FINE FEATHERS 42

FABULOUS FINCH 44

IT FITS THE BILL 46

BRILLIANT BIRDS 48

THE MIRACLE OF AN EGG 50

BUILDING MARVELS 52

PERCH, WALK AND WADE 54

HUNTERS BY THE SEA 56

USE YOUR EYES 58

OCEAN LIFE

FEEDING THE SEAS 62

MARINE MARVELS 64

FLOWERY FIENDS 66

FANTASTIC FISH 68

WARNING STRIPES 70

BONELESS DWELLERS 72

SMALL BUT DEADLY 74

COLOURFUL CORAL 76

HUNTING FOR A HOME 78

DEEP-SEA MONSTERS ... 80

BRIGHT LIGHTS ... 82

USE YOUR EYES ... 84

PLANTS

ENERGY MACHINES ... 88

TOWERS AND TUBES ... 90

MOSS MOUNTAINS ... 92

TALENTED TREES ... 94

FLOWERS IN FANCY DRESS ... 96

PLANTS ON THE MOVE ... 98

SEED JOURNEYS ... 100

GREEN DEFENDERS ... 102

MEAT-EATING PLANTS ... 104

PLANT PARTNERS ... 106

FRUITING FUNGI ... 108

USE YOUR EYES ... 110

GLOSSARY ... 112

INDEX ... 115

NOTES FOR PARENTS AND TEACHERS ... 118

ZOOM INTO...

...the world of bugs, birds, ocean life and plants, and begin a journey that takes you to hidden places, full of mystery and surprises. With this amazing book you can imagine what it is like to be bug-sized, or what it might be like to have wings, or live under water or even be a microscopic plant. Get ready to discover some fantastic facts and get close to the world in ways you never thought possible. It's time to ZOOM!

Zoom in

Look at an ant, a feather, a leaf or a piece of seaweed through a microscope, or through a camera's **macro lens**, and you will notice that they appear bigger than in real life. A microscope uses lenses to magnify the image of very small things, often several hundred times. Modern microscopes may use other techniques to magnify objects many thousands of times.

Almost real

Pictures with the ACTUAL SIZE icons are shown at their real-life size, as though they're right on the page! Comparing things to a standard paperclip really helps you to understand its size.

ACTUAL SIZE

Macro photography

The art of taking pictures of small things in close-up is called macro photography. Using these, and other techniques, photographers and scientists have helped us to uncover things we never knew existed, by giving us the world in close-up. Images with the ZOOM icon show you how many times things have been magnified.

ZOOM x 10

Try it

WHAT IS IT? images let you use your new investigation skills to guess what the picture might be. Just turn over the page each time to find out the answer!

WHAT IS it?

ZOOM x3

BUGS

READY FOR ACTION

Most bugs are small enough to hide easily. So if your survival depended on finding and catching thousands of them, you would want to be well equipped. **Mantids** have it all – great eyesight, lightning reactions and legs that are covered in gripping spines.

Large eyes at the front of the head, so the mantid can judge how far away prey is.

Front legs are covered in spines to create a trap as the legs fold in on the prey.

ZOOM x9

Wait and see
Most mantids are green, so they can hide from their prey among leaves. They sit absolutely still, but they are alert and ready for action. When a mantid sees lunch approaching, it prepares for attack, and lunges in less than one thousandth of a second – that is about 300 times faster than the blink of an eye.

Praying mantid

ZOOM x3

ZOOM x4

Posed for action

The mantid's front legs are bent, and held in a strange pose that makes it look as if it is praying. In reality, these spiked legs are ready for a much less peaceful activity. Fast and strong, the vice-like limbs can catch and crush an insect in less than a second.

While the front half of the body lunges forwards, the back half stays still.

FACTOID

Some mantids are big enough to hunt for larger prey. They can attack birds and lizards.

VITAL STATISTICS

Common name	Praying mantid
Latin name	*Mantidae*
Size	12–150 mm in length
Habitat	Forests
Special feature	Lightning-quick predator

Leafy insects

*This giant leaf insect has **camouflaged** itself by pretending to be part of a plant. When an animal pretends to be something else, it is called a mimic. Look closely to see this bug has fake 'veins' and brown edges, just like a real leaf.*

GROWING UP

Look deep into the world of bugs and you will find incredible changes occur as their **lifecycles** unfold. Take an ugly blowfly as an example. With its big eyes, bristly body and shiny green **cuticle**, this fly is easy to recognize. But would you recognize its young so easily?

◄ Blowflies with a green metallic sheen are called greenbottles.

ZOOM x 14

All change

*Most bugs begin life looking completely different to the way they will look as adults. They go through extraordinary changes as they grow. Each change is a **metamorphosis** – which means 'transform shape'.*

The blowfly's life cycle

1 *A female blowfly can smell a dead body, open wound or meat. Within minutes, she arrives to lay about 250 eggs on it. Just 24 hours later, the eggs hatch into tiny **grubs**, called maggots or **larvae**.*

2 *The maggots feed on the flesh or food and as they grow, they **moult**. After two moults, the maggots are much bigger and will soon be ready to metamorphose.*

3 *Each maggot grows a tough, dark case around its body and becomes a **pupa**.*

4 *It takes at least six days for the pupa to transform into an adult. When the pupa breaks open, an adult blowfly emerges.*

Silky case

Some bugs wrap themselves in a silk **cocoon** when they pupate. They make the silk in special silk glands in their bodies. The larvae of silkworm moths are kept in large farms, and the silk from their cocoons is used to weave silk for clothing.

Stripping off

When a bug grows, it gets too big for its tough skin, or cuticle. The simple solution is to strip off the old skin – this is called moulting – to reveal a new, bigger cuticle underneath.

ZOOM x 12

ACTUAL SIZE

Giant grubs

The larva of a Hercules beetle can reach up to 16 centimetres long and weigh 150 grams, making it one of the largest grubs in the world. It feeds on soft, rotting wood.

WHAT IS IT?

ZOOM x 160

BIG-EYED BUGS

How great would your eyesight be if your eyes covered your whole head? Members of the dragonfly family are lucky enough to have enormous eyes and great vision. Their eyesight is so good, these insects can see in almost every direction. They can see colours (except red) and even **ultraviolet** light, which is a type of light that humans cannot see.

With thousands of lenses in each eye, the dragonfly can spot the slightest movement.

Like all insects, the dragonfly has six legs.

A trick of the light

*The Southern Hawker dragonfly has 30,000 **lenses** in each eye. A lens focuses light that enters the eyes, and nerves carry the image to the brain. There, the brain takes all 60,000 images and turns them into a fantastic ability to see. Insect eyes are especially good at detecting movement. Human eyes have just one lens each – but the quality of images that our brains can see is much better.*

ZOOM x14

Strong, transparent wings make this insect a powerful flier.

Air acrobatics

Members of the dragonfly family aren't just superb at seeing, they are also among the world's best fliers. They can twist and turn each of their long, lacy wings independently, so they can fly forwards, backwards, change direction quickly and even hover.

ZOOM x13

Elongated body

Dragonfly

ZOOM x5

FACTOID

Prehistoric dragonflies were enormous, with a wingspan of 75 centimetres!

VITAL STATISTICS

Common name	Southern Hawker dragonfly
Latin name	*Aeshna cyanea*
Size	70 mm in length
Habitat	Near ponds and rivers, in gardens and woodlands
Special feature	Superb flier

It is...

the larva of a dragonfly. These youngsters are called nymphs (say: nimfs) and they live in water, where they hunt worms, tadpoles and even small fish. They have jaw-like pincers on their head, which they use to grab their prey.

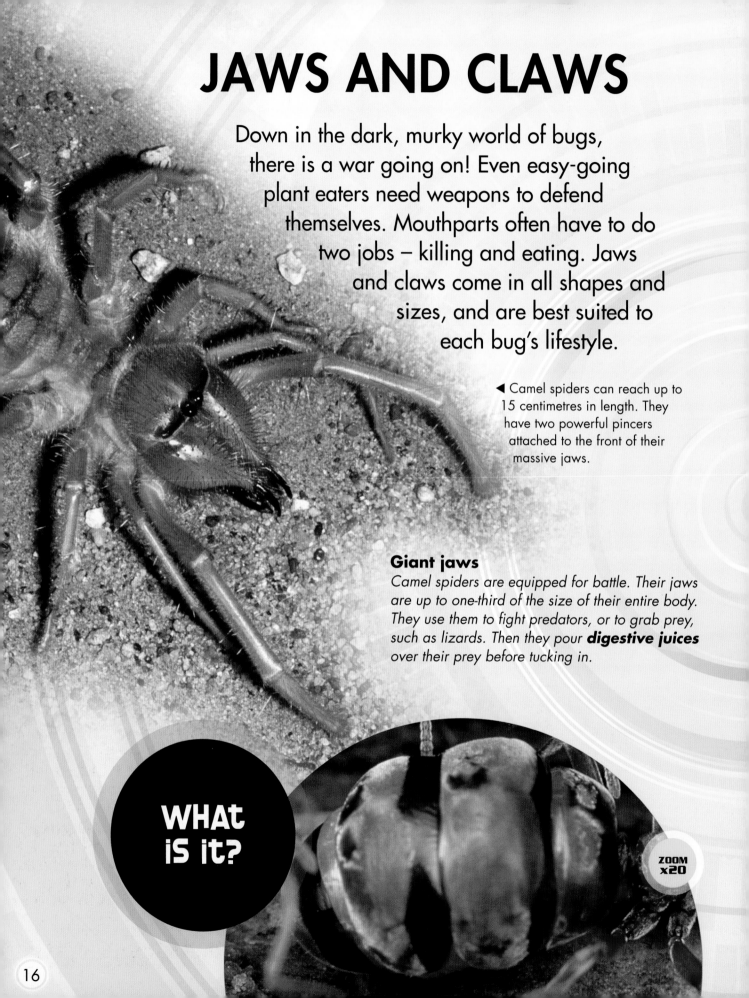

JAWS AND CLAWS

Down in the dark, murky world of bugs, there is a war going on! Even easy-going plant eaters need weapons to defend themselves. Mouthparts often have to do two jobs – killing and eating. Jaws and claws come in all shapes and sizes, and are best suited to each bug's lifestyle.

◄ Camel spiders can reach up to 15 centimetres in length. They have two powerful pincers attached to the front of their massive jaws.

Giant jaws
*Camel spiders are equipped for battle. Their jaws are up to one-third of the size of their entire body. They use them to fight predators, or to grab prey, such as lizards. Then they pour **digestive juices** over their prey before tucking in.*

WHAT IS IT?

ZOOM x20

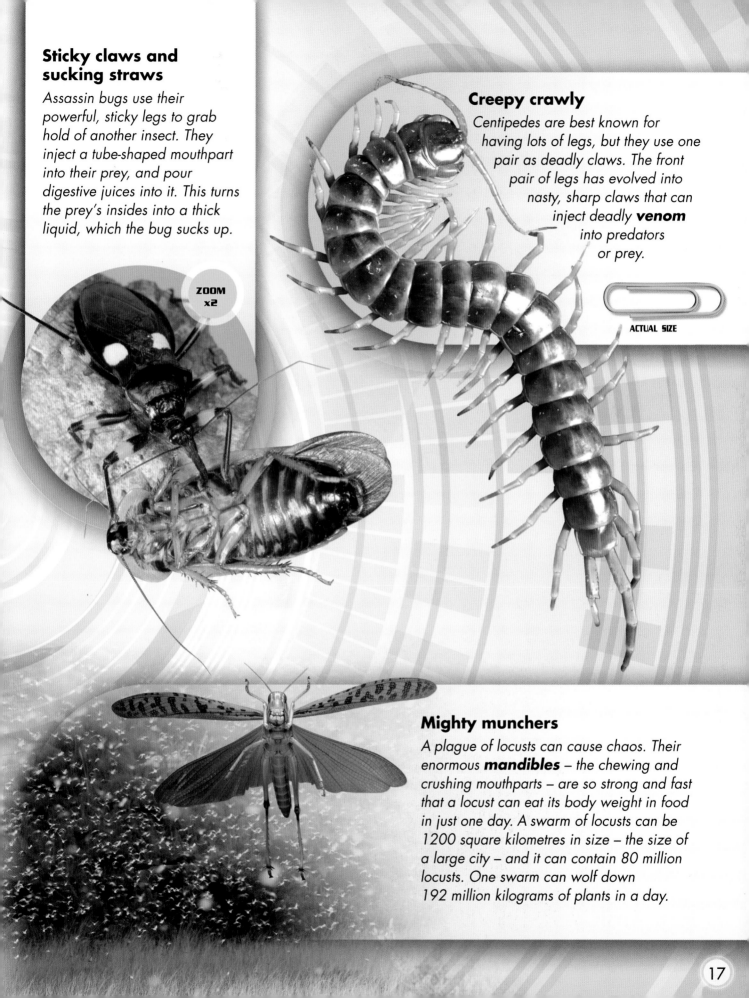

Sticky claws and sucking straws

Assassin bugs use their powerful, sticky legs to grab hold of another insect. They inject a tube-shaped mouthpart into their prey, and pour digestive juices into it. This turns the prey's insides into a thick liquid, which the bug sucks up.

ZOOM x2

Creepy crawly

Centipedes are best known for having lots of legs, but they use one pair as deadly claws. The front pair of legs has evolved into nasty, sharp claws that can inject deadly **venom** into predators or prey.

ACTUAL SIZE

Mighty munchers

A plague of locusts can cause chaos. Their enormous **mandibles** – the chewing and crushing mouthparts – are so strong and fast that a locust can eat its body weight in food in just one day. A swarm of locusts can be 1200 square kilometres in size – the size of a large city – and it can contain 80 million locusts. One swarm can wolf down 192 million kilograms of plants in a day.

ANTS UNITED

The menacing face of an ant hides a brilliant brain. These little bugs have bigger brains than any other insect, with 250,000 brain cells each. Their real intelligence, however, comes from the way ants work together. Scientists think that a **colony** of ants operates like a super-brain. A colony can make decisions, working together in the same way that the cells inside our brains co-ordinate their efforts.

Driver ant

ZOOM
x15

Hooked claws help the ant to climb over plants.

Ready for action
Ants have two main eyes, which can detect movement, and three smaller eyes, called ocelli, which are better at detecting levels of light. Their main sense, however, is smell. Strong jaws, or mandibles, can be used to tear and carry food, build nests or bite prey.

ZOOM
x22

It is...

a queen herdsman ant, leading her colony to a new nest. From time to time, a queen decides to lead her whole colony nearer to food supplies, and a new nest is built. The colony may contain more than 10,000 workers and 4000 larvae and pupae.

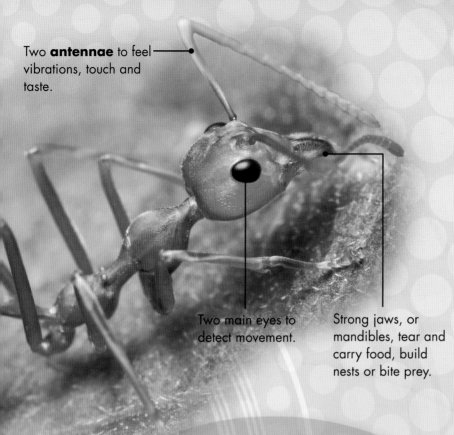

Two **antennae** to feel vibrations, touch and taste.

Two main eyes to detect movement.

Strong jaws, or mandibles, tear and carry food, build nests or bite prey.

FACTOID

Driver ants are the largest ants in the world. Working together, a colony attacks every animal in its path – including snakes and people.

VITAL STATISTICS

Common name	Driver ant
Latin name	*Dorylus nigricans*
Size	5–50 mm in length
Habitat	Rainforests and grasslands
Special feature	Can live in colonies of 20 million ants

ZOOM
x14

Job share

Ants are called social insects because they live and work together. One queen lays all of the colony's eggs. Worker ants are wingless females (left) that do all the chores, including fetching food, nest-building and taking care of the eggs. Male ants grow wings and create swarms at mating time.

19

HIDDEN FROM VIEW

Even with the best camera equipment, or the sharpest eyesight, it can be almost impossible to find some bugs. Look closely at these pictures and be amazed at the many ways nature uses colour, pattern and shape to make an animal disappear from view.

◀ A **katydid**'s camouflage makes it blend into the tree bark, so it isn't seen by prey or predators.

ZOOM x3.5

Singing for your mate
When a bug is cunningly disguised as a leaf or patch of moss, how can it expect its mates to find it? One answer is to sing. Katydids are bush crickets that are masters of deception, but they alert mates to their presence with a loud and characteristic song that sounds like 'katy-she-did'.

WHAT IS it?

ZOOM x2

Prickly problems

When treehoppers suck the tasty sap from inside a plant stem, they could be sitting targets for predators. They overcome this problem by disguising themselves as part of the plant. The young bugs look like the brown, knobbly bark, but the adults pretend they are green prickly thorns instead.

ZOOM
x5

Pretty as a petal

Colourful crab spiders perch motionless on flowers, and calmly wait for lunch to walk by. These lurking predators are invisible because their colours are flawlessly matched to the colours of the petals.

ZOOM
x10

Clever tricks

This trickery certainly works on birds, which normally wouldn't hesitate to swoop down and pluck a fat, juicy caterpillar from its feeding grounds. With a green body, the caterpillar is camouflaged among leaves, but that freaky face on the caterpillar's rear end is enough to make any sharp-eyed predator think twice.

ZOOM
x2

BEAUTIFUL BUGS

Have you ever wondered how butterflies are able to produce such dramatic colours and patterns on their wings? The secret lies in the structure of tiny scales that are able to turn light into incredibly vivid blues, reds and greens. Some butterflies even appear to have a metallic sheen to their wings.

Creating colour
*The overlapping scales on a butterfly's wing can have a range of colour **pigments**, shiny reflective 'mirrors' and air spaces. These work together to absorb ultraviolet light, which our eyes can't see, and turn it into bright patches of blue and green. They work in a similar way to light-emitting diodes (LEDs), which are used in televisions.*

ZOOM x700

Iridescent colours on a butterfly's wings change depending on the angle that you view them.

It is...

an owl butterfly, flaunting its eerie-looking **eye-spot**. The flash of the 'eye', when the butterfly flutters its wings, is startling, and might make a predator think twice before attacking – all the time the butterfly needs to make its escape.

The **proboscis**, or mouthpart, is shaped like a straw, but absorbs liquid.

Peacock butterfly

ZOOM x3

The peacock butterfly's wings make a strange 'hissing' sound when they open to scare away predators.

VITAL STATISTICS

Common name	Peacock butterfly
Latin name	*Inachis io*
Size	50-70 mm (wingspan)
Habitat	Gardens and meadows
Special feature	Four false eyes on wings

Short but sweet

The larvae of butterflies and moths are called caterpillars, and their job is to feed and grow. This caterpillar's stunning skin is a colourful warning that it is covered with stinging bristles. After metamorphosis this impressive little beast will emerge from a cocoon as a drab brown moth.

ZOOM x5

ON THE MOVE

Bugs are amazing. Their hugely adaptable bodies have evolved the ability to move in all types of ways. There are bugs that can fly, ones that crawl and others that can swim. And there are even some that can do all three!

ZOOM X8

◀ Being able to fly is an essential life skill for an emerald euphoria beetle. It moves from flower to flower, eating nectar and pollen.

Gripping force

Spiders are able to crawl over smooth surfaces because they have tufts of tiny hairs under their claws. Each hair is further divided into thousands of tiny 'end feet', which help the spider to stick to the smoothest of surfaces, including glass.

ZOOM x1500

Elastic jumpers

Tiny cat fleas can jump up to 34 centimetres in a single leap, and they can keep jumping for several days without stopping for a rest. Fleas have ultra-elastic material, called resilin, in their legs, which can be squeezed and released like a spring.

ZOOM x30

Fast bugs

Tiger beetles are among the fastest of all bugs. The colourful Australian tiger beetle can chase its insect prey at 9 kilometres an hour, before tearing it apart with large mandibles.

ZOOM x5

ZOOM x3

Swimming and diving

Water boatmen are able to swim and dive, thanks to a special pair of legs, which are shaped like oars. They are long, and fringed with hairs. These bugs can survive underwater because they carry bubbles of air next to their body.

WHAT IS IT?

ZOOM x8

HONEY MONSTERS

Most of us think twice before getting up close and personal to a bee. That buzzing sound, those warning stripes and the fear of being stung are all good ways to keep us – and predators – at arms' length. In fact, bees are among the most important bugs on the planet. Without them, flowers would not grow seeds, and we would quickly run out of food.

The chest area, or thorax, is packed with muscles used for flying.

FACTOID

Bees travel 90,000 kilometres, and visit more than two million flowers, to make a single jar of honey. One honey-bee will produce just half a teaspoon of honey in its whole life.

VITAL STATISTICS

Common name	Honey-bee
Latin name	*Apis mellifera*
Size	0.5–2.5 cm in length
Habitat	Anywhere that flowers grow
Special feature	Are able to turn nectar and pollen from flowers into sweet honey

ZOOM x5

Super storage
Bees have pollen baskets on their legs, which they use to store pollen that they collect from flowers. Worker bees use the pollen to make honey, and to feed the colony.

The legs are covered in small hairs. Pollen sticks to them.

Bee

Sting for protection (females only). If it uses the sting, it will die.

ZOOM x8

Four wings

Home sweet home

A beehive is home to the colony. The queen lays eggs in wax cells, where they are tended by workers. When the eggs hatch, workers feed the larvae. Most of the larvae will grow into workers. Some of them will grow into males, which are called drones. A few will grow into queens.

ZOOM x2

It is...

an orchid bee. These are the only animals, apart from humans, that are known to make perfumes. Males collect scents from orchid flowers and mix them with other ingredients, such as fruit, to make a perfume that attracts females.

SPOTS AND STRIPES

Patterns, spots and stripes decorate many bug bodies. Certain patterns may help a bug to remain hidden in the undergrowth, or they may make them more attractive to mates. Bold patterns and colours are often used to warn predators that the bug tastes foul, or stings.

ZOOM x20

Dressed to impress
*Glamorous male ladybird spiders use their red back, black spots and white-banded legs to impress females, who are dark and dull by comparison. Each female can only lay one **brood** of eggs because when they hatch, the little **spiderlings** gang up and eat her!*

Pretty in peach
Velvet worms have delicate colours, and often patterns on their soft, squidgy body. These animals live in dark, moist habitats and can shoot a jet of slime to catch their prey.

ZOOM x2

Spiral puzzle
Grove snails with light-coloured shells live in warmer places than those with dark shells. No one knows why some grove snails have dark spiral bands, while others have plain shells.

ZOOM x4

WHAT IS IT?

Blue genes
How do bugs create colours and patterns on their bodies? Scientists think it might be the work of a special **protein**, called morphogen. When morphogen reaches certain parts of the bug's body, it tells them to start making pigment, which creates colour. It is the bug's **genes** that decide where the morphogen will have this effect.

ZOOM x 10

ZOOM x 14

29

HAIRY NOT SCARY

Imagine you could shrink to the size of a bird-eating spider, and come face to face with one of these mini-beasts. These are the largest of all spiders, and some of the biggest bugs on the planet. Thankfully, bird-eating spiders – also known as tarantulas – look more deadly than they actually are.

Tarantula

ACTUAL SIZE

Eight eyes – some to detect light and some to detect movement.

Leglike limbs, called pedipalps, are used for touch and to hold prey.

Fangs, called chelicerae, inject venom into prey.

A bad rep

Lots of people are scared of spiders, but they don't deserve their bad reputation. Very few spiders are capable of hurting humans, and spider bites are very rare events. In fact, spiders are incredibly important. They kill flies and other disease-bearing bugs, and are food for billions of other animals, including mammals, birds, reptiles and amphibians.

Spiky hairs on the back

ZOOM x2

Touchy-feely

Spiders have little hairs all over their body. The hairs are essential to a spider's survival. They are extremely sensitive to touch and vibration, so they alert the spider to the presence of another animal nearby. Even blind spiders, such as those that live in caves, can find and catch a fly, just by using this type of information.

Four pairs of legs

FACTOID

Spiders do not have a tongue or a nose. They can smell and taste things by using the special hairs on their legs.

VITAL STATISTICS

Common name	Mexican redknee tarantula
Latin name	*Brachypelma smithi*
Size	13–18 cm in length
Habitat	Scrubland and deserts
Special feature	Can live for more than 20 years

It is...

a female wasp spider, with bright warning stripes. Males are small, brown and easy to miss. These spiders are orb-weavers, which means they create complex webs of silk. They use the webs to catch their prey, which are killed with a venomous bite.

USE YOUR EYES

Study these zooms that appear throughout the Bugs section of your book. Can you recognize any of them just by looking at them? Are there any clues, such as colour, bodyparts or shape, that help you work out where you've seen these images before?

1 As I flutter by you will see flashes of vibrant colour.

2 I pray for my supper, but beware my striking pose. Who am I?

3 I am a giant Scolopendran, but you know me better by my common name.

4 I am a desert fighter with mighty mandibles.

5 I am the sweetest of bugs with a sting in the tail.

6 Cats might think I am an irritating pest.

7 I spend all of my time eating and growing. When I grow up, I want to be a giant beetle, with legs and wings.

8 My name could fool you. I'm no lady and I have eight legs, not six (or even two!).

9 Who are you looking at? This giant eye is a clever trick.

11 My eyes are bigger than my brain but are you smart enough to name me?

10 You could get dizzy following my lovely spiral.

Answers: 1. p23 2. p10 3. p17 4. p16 5. p26 6. p25 7. p13 8. p28 9. p21 10. p29 11. p14

BIRDS

SILENT BUT DEADLY

The feathers on an owl's face help to focus sound towards its ears.

Owls are the silent hunters of the night. Under cover of darkness, they swoop through the forest, searching for small animals to eat. With superb eyesight, they can spot the smallest movement and quietly move in for the kill.

Owl

Eyes to the front
While most birds have eyes on the sides of their head, owls have eyes that face forwards. Forward-facing eyes are better for focusing on prey, to judge both distance and the speed of movement.

ACTUAL SIZE

These owls fly with soft, slow wingbeats, often close to the ground.

The bill is usually hooked and sharp for tearing at meat.

Feathers are often coloured to provide camouflage.

Softly, softly

Owls have soft **downy** feathers on their body and feet. These help to muffle the noise of their wings in flight, and means they can approach their prey in silence. Feathers around their ears help direct sound straight into the ear canal.

ACTUAL SIZE

FACTOID

Eurasian eagle owls are huge, with a wingspan of 2 metres. They can attack and kill foxes, small deer and other large owls.

VITAL STATISTICS

Common name	Eurasian eagle owl
Latin name	*Bupo bupo*
Size	58–70 cm in length
Habitat	Forests, grasslands and deserts
Special feature	Calls "ouho-oohu-oohu"

Owl pellets

Owls can't digest all of the bones, claws, fur and teeth they swallow. These hard bits are collected in part of the bird's stomach, then brought up and coughed out of the mouth as a pellet, called an owl pellet.

HIGH FLIERS

Even with a pair of binoculars in your hands, it is hard to imagine how birds fly. Scientists had to zoom in close, and look at how birds' bodies are built, to understand the phenomenon of flight. It is all to do with feathers, wing shape and power.

Why fly?

There are only three types of animals that can truly fly – insects, bats and birds. Flight takes lots of energy, and a specially adapted body, but there are advantages to a life in the air. An animal that flies can explore new areas to live or feed, escape predators and find mates.

▲ A hungry African fish eagle soars above water, looking for fish.

WHAT iS it?

ZOOM x7

Holey bones

Bones can be heavy, so to save weight – and energy – birds have bones that are filled with air. The struts, or bars, of bone keep the structure strong but very light.

ZOOM x25

Flap and lift

Birds need two forces to fly – lift, which raises them off the ground, and thrust, which pushes the bird forwards. They achieve this by flapping their wings. These limbs are shaped so air moves over the top and bottom at different speeds, which helps to lift the bird up, and then move it forwards.

Ways to fly

Birds change the way they move their wings and their flapping speed to fly, soar, accelerate or swoop. When a kingfisher dives into water, its eyes are focused upon a fish. It spreads its wing and tail feathers to slow down as it enters the water. With a fish in its bill, the kingfisher will shoot out of the water, and fly to a tree to devour its prey.

SPEEDY WINGS

Little hummingbirds are like flying gems of the forest. They zip and dart through the air, visiting up to 2000 **tropical** flowers a day to feed at lightning speed. This way of life is so exhausting that hummingbirds spend most of their time asleep or resting!

Beating its wings 50 times every single minute enables the bird to hover, but it burns energy fast.

Air acrobats

These birds can feed at flowers by hovering – flying while staying in one place. Hummingbirds achieve this incredible feat by moving their wings in a figure-of-eight rather than flapping them up and down.

ACTUAL SIZE

It is...

a hummingbird nest. These little birds lay the smallest eggs, with some no bigger than a pea. The nests and eggs of some hummingbirds are so small and well hidden that they have never been found.

ZOOM x2

Long, slender bill to reach deep into a flower to get nectar.

Both male and female hummingbirds usually have bright, colourful plumage.

A small body and active lifestyle mean this hummingbird must feed on an energy-rich food source: sugary nectar.

Tiny bee hummingbirds are the smallest birds in the world, with an average wingspan of just 33 millimetres.

VITAL STATISTICS

Common name	Bee hummingbird
Latin name	*Mellisuga helenae*
Size	55–61 mm in length
Habitat	Tropical forests
Special feature	Females lay two pea-sized eggs

Rainbow colours

Hummingbird feathers have a beautiful metallic shimmer, which is called iridescence. The colours are created when light hits the feathers and is bent, or refracted, back in the same way that colours form in the thin film of a soap bubble.

ZOOM x10

FINE FEATHERS

Feathers are super structures that have extraordinary properties. They keep birds dry, warm or cool – and are essential for flight. Feathers are made of **keratin**, which is the same protein you have in your nails and hair.

◄ Male and female grey crowned cranes wear splendid **crests** of stiff, gold feathers.

ACTUAL SIZE

Pretty plumage
A bird's feathers are called its plumage and the colours are a balance between camouflage and attention-seeking. Birds that need to hide from predators often have dull, brown plumage. Others – often male birds – like to show off with fine feathers, bold colours and impressive crests or tails.

ZOOM x120

WHAt iS it?

Zoom a plume

A powerful microscope, called a scanning electron microscope, reveals the incredible structure of a penguin's feather. Orange **barbs** fan out from a central shaft, or **rachis**. Each barb has many tiny hooked filaments, called **barbules**. They hook together, trapping air to keep the bird warm, and helping to make its plumage waterproof.

ZOOM x 100

Feather types

A bird's large, stiff feathers are mostly used for flight, and are found on its wings and tail. Contour feathers, like this one, grow over the bird's body. The barbs overlap, and help to give a bird its streamlined shape. Soft, downy **plumes** near the base of the feather's rachis trap air and insulate the body (keep it warm by preventing the bird's body heat from escaping).

ZOOM x3

Fit for flight

Flight feathers are called ramiges. Primary flight feathers, like these, grow on the wingtips and can be spread out to give the wing a large surface area. A bird can fan its ramiges out, or twist them, to control the direction and speed of flight. Like ramiges, a bird's tail feathers are stiff and can be moved. By dipping and spreading its tail feathers, a bird can rapidly slow down to avoid a crash-landing.

FABULOUS FINCH

Gouldian finches have such colourful feathers, they look as if they have been dipped in paint. These birds live only in parts of northern Australia, where they were once common. Now Gouldian finches are rare and fewer than 250 live in the wild.

Stout, strong bill for cracking open seeds.

Black, red or orange-yellow face

Drab chicks

Gouldian finches may stay with the same mate for life. The chicks have a drab plumage compared to their parents. Until they can fly the nest, the chicks are vulnerable to predators. Flashy feathers would be like wearing an 'Eat me' sign!

ACTUAL SIZE

Gouldian finch

ZOOM x2

It is...

a bird feather louse, a type of **parasite**, nestled between feather barbs. Some bird parasites eat feathers; others suck blood. Gouldian finches suffer from burrowing mite parasites, which feed on their skin.

Brightly coloured plumage

Males have longer tails than females.

FACTOID

Sixty years ago, there were millions of Gouldian finches. They are so rare because many have been captured to be kept in cages, and their forest habitat has been destroyed.

VITAL STATISTICS

Common name	Gouldian finch
Latin name	*Erythrura gouldiae*
Size	13 cm in length
Habitat	Grasslands and forests
Special feature	Incredible colours

ZOOM x2

Handsome hawfinch
The plumage of this male hawfinch will impress any females nearby. These finches live in cooler places than Gouldian finches, and balance the need for fine feathers with an ability to hide from predators in dense woodlands. Their tough bills can break open olive and cherry stones.

IT FITS THE BILL

When you look closely at a bird, pay particular attention to the shape and size of its bill. This tough, toothless mouth can tell you more about how the bird lives its life than any other body part. A bill grows from a bird's skull, and it keeps growing throughout a bird's life. It is constantly worn away, so it doesn't get any bigger in an adult bird.

ACTUAL SIZE

Big mouth
Toucans have huge, colourful bills. These tropical birds don't need big bills for their diet of fruit and insects, so why carry around such big mouths? No one knows, although a big bill may work like a giant air-conditioning unit, helping the birds to stay cool.

WHAT IS it?

ZOOM x4

Small but strong

Cone-shaped bills are particularly strong near the base. They are the perfect shape for tackling hard nuts, and getting through a tough skin and into the soft flesh of a fruit. This greenfinch uses its cone-shaped bill to crack open sunflower seeds.

Keeping a safe distance

Birds that eat insects often have tweezer-like bills. The bills are often long, to keep a bird safe from stings or bites. Bee-eaters grab their prey in their bills, and hit them against a branch until they have released their sting.

Table manners

Birds of prey, such as this white-tailed eagle, tear at meat. These huge birds **scavenge**, which means they feed on dying or dead animals. A long bill helps to keep bacteria and blood away from their feathers, eyes and nostrils.

BRILLIANT BIRDS

African grey parrots are super smart birds. In fact, they are so clever, some people think that they are as intelligent as whales, apes and even young children! Parrots are noisy, colourful birds that live in large groups, or colonies.

Bare skin around yellow eye

Sharp, hooked bill

Unusual feeding

Parrots, such as this scarlet macaw, use their feet like hands, grabbing hold of food to bring it up to their mouth. Blue hyacinth macaws eat tough palm nuts. They often pick nuts out of cow dung because they are easier to eat after they have been through a cow's digestive system!

ACTUAL SIZE

It is...

a hill mynah. These glossy birds are famous for their ability to mimic, or copy, human voices. Parrots not only mimic; they can learn the meaning of some words.

Light fantastic

The colours of parrot feathers are unique, and are created in a way shared by no other birds. Parrot feathers scatter light, and contain unusual pigments (substances that create colour) to produce vivid blues, greens and reds.

ACTUAL SIZE

Grey feathers with white edges

Grey parrot

Adults are not as colourful as many other parrots, but they do have cherry-red tail feathers.

FACTOID

Members of the parrot family can live long lives – up to 80 years. However, this group of birds is threatened with extinction.

VITAL STATISTICS

Common name	African grey parrot
Latin name	*Psittacus erithacus*
Size	33 cm in length
Habitat	Lowland tropical forest
Special feature	Talkative

THE MIRACLE OF AN EGG

Female birds lay eggs, and most parent birds look after their chicks as they grow. If you could look inside an egg, and watch a chick develop, you would observe one of nature's most incredible events.

ACTUAL SIZE

◀ It took about 21 days for this baby chicken to develop inside its egg. Smaller birds, such as sparrows, can hatch in less than two weeks.

A chick's life cycle

1 **Membranes** keep liquids in the egg, and allow gases to pass through the shell. The yellow yolk contains food for the growing chick.

2 The shell gets thinner as the chick grows. The calcium it contains is used to build the chick's skeleton. Egg white (albumen) protects the chick, and provides food.

3 Chicks have a small 'tooth' on their bill, which they use to crack open the shell.

4 A newly hatched chick has damp feathers, but they soon dry to become soft and fluffy.

Grow zone

Eggs contain all the goodness a growing chick will need before it hatches. However, the chicks need to be kept warm to develop. This means the parents have to sit on the eggs – it is a process called incubation.

ACTUAL SIZE

Hens lay eggs

All female birds are called hens, not just chickens. The eggs are developing inside the body even before the hens mate with the male birds. The male birds fertilize the eggs during mating.

Feed me!

Chicks can open their large mouths extra wide. They rely on their parents to bring food to them while they grow. When they are ready to fly, they are called fledglings.

ZOOM x4

WHAT IS IT?

ACTUAL SIZE

BUILDING MARVELS

Weavers are the best builders in the bird world. They build the most extraordinary nests. Look closely, and you will see that they don't just pile bits of plants on top of each other – they actually weave them together to create an elaborate and strong fortress.

Grasses or reeds are woven together to create the nest walls.

ZOOM x2

Mud and spit
Swallows build their nests with mud and spit then line it with soft straw and feathers. Tucked away in their cup-shaped nest, these barn swallow chicks can feed and grow, while staying out of danger from predators.

FACTOID

Cape weavers sometimes build nests that hang from branches above water, where few predators can reach them. But if the water level rises, the nest will flood and the chicks will drown.

VITAL STATISTICS

Common name	Cape weaver
Latin name	*Ploceus capensis*
Size	18 cm in length
Habitat	Woodlands
Special feature	Superb nest builders

The nest entrance is usually a tunnel.

Watch me!
Male satin bowerbirds decorate their bowers with any blue or yellow objects they can find. The bower is like a stage, where the males dance and display for females.

The male builds the nest, then sings and dances to entice females to inspect his handiwork.

Weaver bird

It is...

an Emperor penguin chick. There are no nest-building materials in its Antarctic home, so the parents hold the egg, and then the chick, on their feet to keep it warm.

The nest is built between two supports, such as branches or thick grass stems.

PERCH, WALK AND WADE

You can tell a lot about a bird by looking at its feet. Just as a close-up view of a bird's bill will give you clues about its diet, zooming in on a bird's lower limbs will tell you something about where, and how, it lives.

◄ A close-up of a white-tailed eagle as it swoops in for the kill reveals the power of this mighty predator.

Non-slip feet

Birds of prey grab hold of squirming creatures, so they need strong, clawed **talons** *to grip tightly. White-tailed eagles pluck slippery fish out of water but they are also equipped to hunt mammals and other birds, and to scavenge.*

WHAT IS It?

ZOOM x2

ACTUAL SIZE

Waterbirds

Birds, such as coots, that wade through shallow water looking for small animals to eat often have long slender legs. Their feet have long toes that are spread far apart, to stop the bird from sinking into mud. Swimming birds, such as ducks and penguins, have webbed feet. Webbing helps them to move through water with speed and power.

ZOOM x2

Sleep tight

Perching birds, or passerines, have three toes pointing forwards on each foot, and one toe pointing behind. This arrangement means a passerine can grip tightly on to a branch, even when it is asleep.

Big kickers

Ostriches are huge birds that can run at speeds of 70 kilometres an hour, but cannot fly. They have just two large, fat toes on each foot and are able to kick with enough force to kill a lion.

55

HUNTERS BY THE SEA

Puffins are one of the world's strangest-looking birds. They have been called 'sea parrots' and 'clowns of the ocean' because of their comical face and coloured bill. These striking seabirds are not great fliers, but their swimming and hunting skills are awesome.

Grey or white face

Strong, conical bill

Puffin

Brightly coloured bill in summer – with blue, red and yellow parts.

ZOOM x2

All at sea
Puffins are fearless swimmers in the open oceans, paddling with their large orange webbed feet. They can dive deep below the surface, as far as 20 metres, in pursuit of prey and can stay there for up to 30 seconds at a time.

It is...

the egg of a guillemot. These seabirds lay their eggs directly on to a bare cliff edge, with no nest to protect them. The unusual shape of the egg prevents it from rolling off.

Unusual red and
black eye markings

FACTOID

During the breeding season, a
parent puffin may have to carry its
hoard of food up to 50 kilometres,
back to the nest and hungry chicks.

VITAL STATISTICS

Common name	Atlantic puffin
Latin name	*Fratercula arctica*
Size	27–30 cm in length
Habitat	Sea cliffs and open seas
Special feature	Feed in large groups called rafts

A white breast
and a black body

Ferrying fish

Once a puffin has reached
its prey – usually small
fish – it can catch and hold
several at a time. It does
this by pushing a fish up
with its tongue, onto spikes
on the roof of its mouth.
It can then safely open its
mouth to catch more.

ACTUAL SIZE

USE YOUR EYES

Use your eyes to study these zooms of birds that appear throughout the Birds section. Can you recognize any of them just by looking at them? Are there any clues, such as colour, body parts or shape, that help you work out where you've seen these images before?

1 *I look like I've been dipped in paint.*

2 *Shhh, I've got my eyes on you. I'm a silent hunter, so you won't hear me coming.*

3 *I spread my enormous wings and swoop over water.*

4 *I have brown plumage, but a white tail.*

5 *What yellow bird has been busy weaving this nest?*

6 Two can see better than one, but one can see you!

7 I fly so fast I'm just a beautiful blue blur.

8 I am smart, I can talk and I am handsome, too.

9 Welcome to the world, baby bird!

10 They say I look like a clown or a parrot. Do you agree?

11 Who wants neat feet when you are wading through mud? I like my big feet, but who am I?

Answers: 1. p44–45 2. p36–37 3. p38 4. p47 5. p53 6. p46 7. p41 8. p48 9. p50 10. p57 11. p55

OCEAN LIFE

FEEDING THE SEAS

Plankton are tiny sea creatures that act as food for the ocean's wildlife. They may be small, but they exist in billions. Plankton are eaten by fish and other sea-living creatures, and are at the bottom of the **food chain**. Most plankton live near the surface of the sea, where there is light and warmth. Antarctic krill, however, are tough little creatures.

Large eyes help krill to see in deep, dark water.

Eleven pairs of legs

ZOOM x25

Little and large
See a krill up close and you can make out its tough outer skin, sensory antennae and the special feeding limbs that filter microscopic food from the water. Most Antarctic krill are no bigger than your little finger, yet these creatures live in vast swarms and are the main food for the largest animal that has ever lived – the blue whale.

Transparent
body – light
passes through

Sit or swim

This tiny animal, called an obelia, has a strange lifecycle. It spends part of its life attached to the seabed, and then reaches this jellyfish stage, called a medusa, and can swim. It may become food for other, larger animals.

ZOOM x100

Krill

ZOOM x6

Tough outer skin,
called a carapace

FACTOID

Krill can live in deep water, 4 kilometres below the surface, where there is no light and the water pressure would crush human bones in an instant.

VITAL STATISTICS

Common name	Antarctic krill
Latin name	*Euphausia superba*
Size	1–14 cm in length
Habitat	Throughout oceans
Special feature	Feed on tiny plants

Amazing plankton

This radiolarian is a type of plankton. Most radiolarians are too small to be seen with the naked eye. This one lived many millions of years ago and has been fossilized – turned to stone – over time.

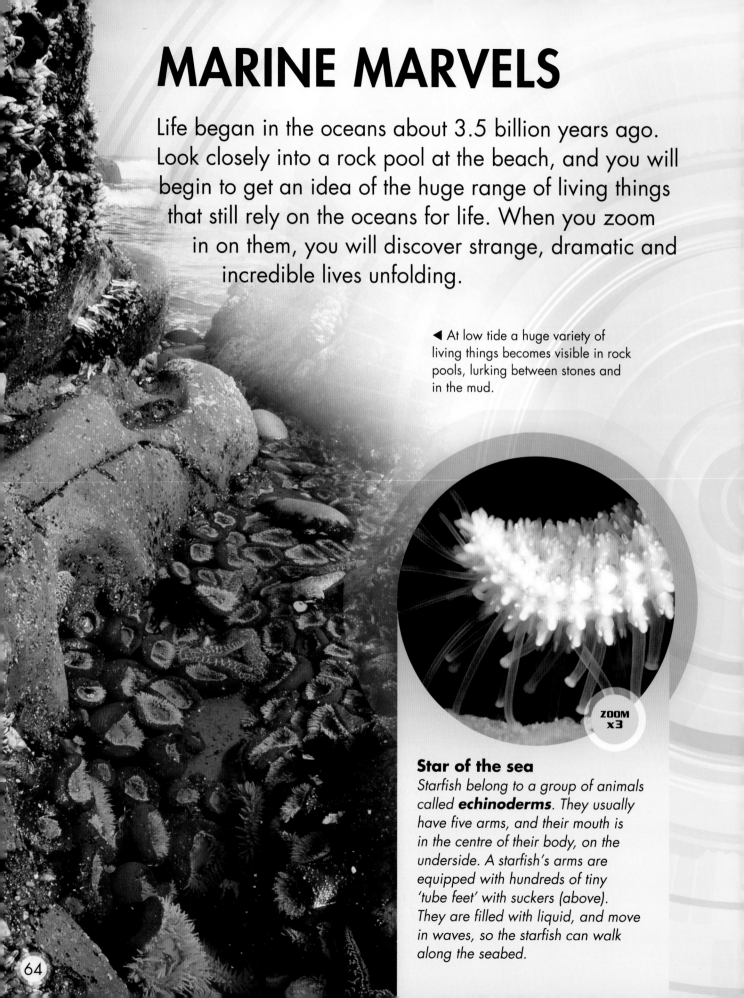

MARINE MARVELS

Life began in the oceans about 3.5 billion years ago. Look closely into a rock pool at the beach, and you will begin to get an idea of the huge range of living things that still rely on the oceans for life. When you zoom in on them, you will discover strange, dramatic and incredible lives unfolding.

◀ At low tide a huge variety of living things becomes visible in rock pools, lurking between stones and in the mud.

ZOOM x3

Star of the sea
*Starfish belong to a group of animals called **echinoderms**. They usually have five arms, and their mouth is in the centre of their body, on the underside. A starfish's arms are equipped with hundreds of tiny 'tube feet' with suckers (above). They are filled with liquid, and move in waves, so the starfish can walk along the seabed.*

Caring for eggs

This tiny sea horse has just hatched from its egg. When a female sea horse lays her eggs, the male scoops them up and keeps them in a special pouch. The eggs grow here until they are ready to hatch, so they are kept safe from predators.

ZOOM x30

Catching a ride

Goose barnacles are animals that are attached to rocks and feed on plankton. A long time ago, it was thought they grew into geese, which is how they got their strange name.

ZOOM x1.5

Spiky stones

Sea urchins look like spiky stones and are a type of echinoderm. They often have venom (poison) in their spines and in their mouth, which is on their bottom! Some tropical urchins have spines that are one centimetre thick.

ACTUAL SIZE

WHAT IS IT?

ZOOM x3

65

FLOWERY FIENDS

Jewel anemones look like beautiful underwater flowers, but they are poisonous predators. When clusters of jewel anemones live on the seafloor or on rocks, they create a carpet of brightly coloured animals. They range in colour from pink to blue and green, but their good looks hide a deadly secret.

Three rings of tentacles

ZOOM
x5

Jewel anemones

ZOOM
x8

Hidden weapons
This beautiful jewel anemone has stings in its stubby tentacles. When fish or other animals swim through the tentacles, the stings are fired at the prey, injecting painful venom. Some anemones have stings that work like harpoons, catching and dragging the prey to the animal's mouth.

100 tentacles around the central cavity – the mouth

Stuck still

Anemones are sessile animals – they are attached to the seabed and rarely move. If they do move, it is very slowly. This tube anemone has a long slender body that is actually buried beneath the seabed. Some tube anemones have bodies that extend down 40 centimetres or more in the sand, mud or gravel.

ZOOM x2

FACTOID

Boxer crabs carry stinging sea anemones on their claws and wave them at any animals they want to scare!

VITAL STATISTICS

Common name	Jewel anemone
Latin name	*Corynactis species*
Size	1 cm across base
Habitat	Shallow water
Special feature	Can divide itself in two

The body is tube-like and has no bones and no shell.

It is...

a clown fish. These fish live in close harmony with some types of sea anemone. The anemone protects them from predators and they feed on small animals that might harm the anemone.

FANTASTIC FISH

What is a fish? There are so many types, in so many shapes, sizes and colours, that it is hard to say exactly what makes a fish. The tiniest ocean fish are smaller than your fingernail, but the largest ones – whale sharks – grow up to 14 metres long.

ZOOM x88

◀ When a shark's skin is magnified, its extraordinary structure becomes visible. Each of these pointed scales is called a denticle and is more similar to a tooth than an ordinary fish scale.

WHAT IS IT?

Baby fish

Few fish look after their eggs or young. A brown trout female can lay 10,000 eggs at a time, in the hope that a few baby fish – called **fry** – make it to adulthood. Eggs and fry are a tasty, nutritious food for many other marine animals.

ZOOM x30

Big eyes

When divers swim up close to glasseye snappers, they get an eyeful. These night-time hunters are fish with superb vision, thanks to their huge eyes. They can grow up to 50 centimetres long and live around reefs.

Deep breathing

Seawater contains **oxygen** – the gas that fish breathe to release energy from food. Water goes into a fish's mouth and flows over its **gills**, which are located behind its head. This image of gills has been magnified to show how they have a large surface area to increase the movement of oxygen into the fish's blood. A waste gas, carbon dioxide, passes out.

ZOOM x250

WARNING STRIPES

The dorsal fins carry venom, or poison.

When deepsea photographers want to take snaps of a lionfish, they are more likely to zoom out than zoom in! These good-looking fish don't wear their stripes for fun – they send out a clear signal that warns other animals to stay away, because those spines can hurt.

Small and spiky

The red stripes on a banded coral shrimp may help this little **crustacean** *to hide, or they may warn hungry lionfish that the shrimp has a surprise in store. Look closely at its back and you will notice a row of sharp spines.*

ACTUAL SIZE

Red-and-white stripes are a warning to predators to stay away.

It is...

a mackerel. The smooth scales on its shiny body reflect light. When a shoal of thousands of mackerel dart through the ocean they create a bright sheet of shimmering light, which confuses their predators.

Fins on the side of the body – pectoral fins – are used to trap prey against rocks or coral.

Lionfish

Some sharks prey on lionfish – the stinging spines have no bad effects on them.

VITAL STATISTICS

Common name	Lionfish
Latin name	*Pterois* species
Size	Up to 40 cm in length
Habitat	Coastal waters in warm places
Special feature	Venomous spines

Can you see me?

A tiny anemone shrimp is easy to miss. It has an almost transparent body, which means it can hide itself between an anemone's tentacles, or among this white coral. When you are small and defenceless, it is a good idea to use your appearance to blend in, or disappear from view – and you just might avoid being eaten by something bigger.

ZOOM x 15

BONELESS DWELLERS

Animals can grow big, soft and squashy in the ocean. This is because water is thicker, or denser, than air and can support an animal's body without the need for lots of bones. Animals without bones are called **invertebrates**, and while some of them grow a tough outer skin or shell for defence, others are soft.

◄ The flamingo tongue snail has soft, patterned skin, which it wraps over its shell. It feeds on sea fans – a type of coral.

ZOOM x5

Mighty molluscs
*Sea slugs and snails belong to a group of animals called **molluscs**, and most of them live in the sea. From shelled mussels at the beach, to mighty squid in the deep ocean, molluscs have become the masters of the marine habitat. There are at least 50,000 different types, or species, of mollusc.*

WHAT is it?

Record breaker

The longest animal ever found was an ocean worm. It was a bootlace worm and measured 55 metres in length. This ragworm grows to a mere 40 centimetres, but it looks fearsome when magnified. It has four small eyes, and two clusters of four tentacles on either side of its head.

Spectacular spiral

This colourful spiral is part of a marine worm, called a Christmas tree worm. Most of its body is out of view, enclosed by a shell-like tube. This spiral is an **organ** with two jobs – it operates like gills, allowing the worm to breathe, and it captures small particles of food that might drift by.

ZOOM x8

ZOOM x2

ACTUAL SIZE

Deadly venom

Cone shells look harmless, but they fire a harpoon loaded with venom that is powerful enough to stun and kill a person. Scientists who study the venom from these marine snails hope to use it to produce painkilling medicines.

SMALL BUT DEADLY

A blue-ringed octopus may be small, but it is deadly – with a 'hazard' warning sign to match. Zoom in close and look at those bold blue rings. They show that the octopus is feeling threatened, and is ready to attack. Its saliva, or spit, contains fast-acting venom that can kill.

ACTUAL SIZE

Blue-ringed octopus

Yellow or light-brown skin

Toxic spike
Zoom up as close as you like to a deadly stonefish, and it may still be invisible. This camouflaged fish is one of the most venomous animals in the world. If you tread on one of 13 spines on its back you could be injected with venom that causes excruciating pain, and even death.

It is...
a giant clam. These molluscs are up to 150 centimetres in length, and do not move from the seabed. They filter small particles of food from seawater and live in the shallow waters of the Pacific Ocean.

This area contains the organs, including a brain, three hearts, two kidneys and a poison gland.

Blue rings appear when the octopus feels threatened.

Eight arms to walk and grab hold of things.

The arms are covered with two rows of suckers.

VITAL STATISTICS

Common name	Blue-ringed octopus
Latin name	*Hapalochlaena* species
Size	10 – 20 cm in length
Habitat	Tropical areas of Pacific and Indian Oceans
Special feature	Bright-blue 'warning' rings

ACTUAL SIZE

Feast or famine?

Blue-ringed octopuses feast on fish, shrimp and crabs. They bite their victim, or release poisonous saliva into the water around it. The octopus waits for the venom to take effect, then eats the prey. This mother octopus will not eat for six months while she protects her white, oval-shaped eggs. When they hatch, she will die.

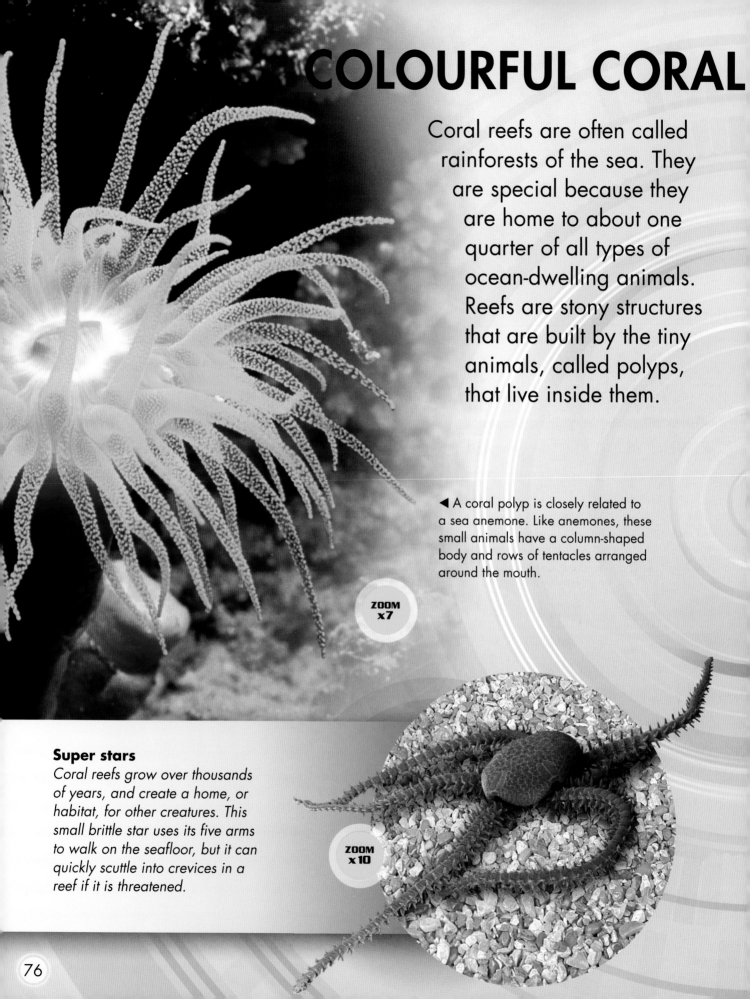

COLOURFUL CORAL

Coral reefs are often called rainforests of the sea. They are special because they are home to about one quarter of all types of ocean-dwelling animals. Reefs are stony structures that are built by the tiny animals, called polyps, that live inside them.

◄ A coral polyp is closely related to a sea anemone. Like anemones, these small animals have a column-shaped body and rows of tentacles arranged around the mouth.

ZOOM x7

Super stars
Coral reefs grow over thousands of years, and create a home, or habitat, for other creatures. This small brittle star uses its five arms to walk on the seafloor, but it can quickly scuttle into crevices in a reef if it is threatened.

ZOOM x10

Hide and seek

Look closely at this coral, and try to find the soft coral crab that is hiding among its branches. Two little beady black eyes are the only clue it is present. The world's first coral reefs grew around 210 million years ago. These warm-water corals grow only in shallow, clean ocean water. The largest reef is the Great Barrier Reef, Australia. It took about 18 million years to grow and is now about 2000 kilometres long.

ACTUAL SIZE

Reefs in danger

Scientists examine coral to find out how reef habitats are changing. In recent times, large areas of reef have changed dramatically. When polyps die, the stony structures they live in turn white, and are described as 'bleached'. It is thought that pollution and **global warming** may cause even larger areas of coral to die.

ACTUAL SIZE

WHAt iS it?

ACTUAL SIZE

HUNTING FOR A HOME

Little hermit crabs are a coral reef's clean-up brigade. They scuttle over rocky surfaces, picking up little bits of food to nibble. This helps the coral polyps to grow and stay healthy. Zoom in close to get a good look at this creature's extraordinary features.

ACTUAL SIZE

Jointed legs for walking and swimming

Hermit crab

FACTOID

Many crabs are scavengers and feed on dead animals. They also hunt, and may lose a claw during a battle. Thankfully, crabs can grow new legs to replace ones they lose.

VITAL STATISTICS

Common name	Scarlet reef hermit crab
Latin name	*Paguristes cadenati*
Size	4 cm (legspan)
Habitat	Coral reefs
Special feature	Lives in a borrowed shell

ZOOM x20

Time to grow
This is one of thousands of eggs laid by the horseshoe crab. The larva is growing inside, and it will take up to ten years for this animal to become an adult.

Eyes are
on stalks.

Sensitive antennae
for touch and to
sense chemicals in
the water or air.

A pair of
strong claws

All change
When crab larvae hatch from
their eggs they look nothing
like their tough-skinned, long-
limbed parents. This little crab
larva will swim with other
plankton and feed by trapping
food in its bristles. As it grows,
it will sink to the seabed and
remain hidden while its hard
skin develops.

ZOOM
x60

It is...

a spotted jellyfish that
lives in the South Pacific.
These animals are related to
coral polyps, and have stinging
tentacles. They are weak
swimmers, and are carried
along by sea currents.

DEEP-SEA MONSTERS

The deeper you dive into the oceans, the darker it gets. At depths of about 200 metres, very little light can filter through, and at depths of 1000 metres, the ocean is inky-black. Zoom down into the deepest ocean zones and you'll find some of the world's most bizarre animals in extreme habitats.

ACTUAL SIZE

◀ A young glass squid is called a larva and lives near the ocean's surface with other plankton. This adult, however, survives in deep, dark water to depths of 2800 metres.

Red jelly

Ocean explorers use robots and remotely operated vehicles (ROVs) to zoom into the deepest places. They have discovered extraordinary animals, such as this small red jellyfish with its thousands of tentacles.

ZOOM x2

Under pressure

Water is 850 times denser than air, which means it is very heavy. This hatchet fish lives in deep oceans and it has to cope with the enormous pressure exerted on its body by the weight of water above it. Every night, however, it swims about 1000 metres to feed on plankton at the ocean's surface.

ZOOM x2

ACTUAL SIZE

Ocean hotspots

In the deep ocean, there are cracks on the seabed, where heat from the inside of the planet escapes. They are called hydrothermal vents, and weird animals live here that can survive nowhere else on Earth, such as these giant tube worms (above).

WHAT IS IT?

BRIGHT LIGHTS

The deep ocean contains many mysteries, but marine scientists are discovering new animals all of the time. One of the most incredible discoveries is the viperfish. These are powerful, fierce predators with a body that is perfectly suited to their deep-sea habitat.

ACTUAL SIZE

Large head

Long, thin and very sharp fangs

Lines of photophores on the underside

ZOOM x4

Glowing in the dark

*Who needs the Sun's light when you can make your own? Some deep-water animals, including viperfish, have special organs in their body, called **photophores**, which make light. These help to confuse predators, or attract prey and mates.*

The lure contains photophores and attracts prey.

Long, thin body

Glowing ribbons
This strange-looking animal is called a comb jelly. Its ribbon-like body is covered on one side with tiny hairs, called cilia. Known as Venus's girdle, this animal swims with a snake-like movement and glows greenish-gold at night.

Viperfish

FACTOID

A female hatchet fish is big, but her partner is tiny. He stays stuck to her body, feeding off her, and fertilizing her eggs.

VITAL STATISTICS

Common name	Viperfish
Latin name	*Chauliodus* species
Size	Up to 30 cm in length
Habitat	At depths of 500–1000 metres
Special feature	Can make its own light

It is...
a deepwater dumbo octopus. Its tentacles are covered with small bristles called cirri. When the cirri move backwards and forwards they create water currents that drag food into the octopus's mouth.

USE YOUR EYES

Use your eyes to study these zooms that appear throughout the Ocean Life section. Can you recognize any of the animals or plants just by looking at these pictures? Are there any clues that help you work out where you've seen these images before?

1 I am too soft to survive, so I borrow someone else's home.

2 I have a long journey to find food, but my body is up to the challenge.

3 I'm small but deadly, so beware my rings of blue.

4 I walk with my arms, how strange is that?

5 My cousins can grow up to 55 metres. I'm smaller, but just as fearsome!

6 Which 'fish' has both arms and feet? That's me!

7 I have a bad temper and spines to match. Divers beware!

8 Giant blue whales make a meal of me.

9 I am named after a large water bird, but I can't fly anywhere.

10 My cousins are slugs and snails, would you believe it?

11 If you see my fangs, you are in deep water!

Answers: 1. p78 2. p81 3. p74–75 4. p76 5. p73 6. p64 7. p70–71 8. p62–63 9. p65 10. p72 11. p82

PLANTS

ENERGY MACHINES

We need plants because they take the energy in sunlight and convert it into food. It is a process called **photosynthesis**. While they are performing this fabulous feat, plants make oxygen, which is the gas we use to turn food back into energy. So, without plants, we could neither eat nor breathe!

Volvox

Each Volvox is just one cell.

The colony is held inside a jelly-like wall.

ZOOM x100

The smallest plants
Living things are made up of building blocks called **cells**. *Huge trees are made of billions of cells, but the simplest plants, such as Volvox, are just one cell. These plants are called* **algae** *(say: al-ghee), and they live in water. Millions of strands of the algae Spirogyra (left) create slimy, green pond scum.*

ZOOM
x130

One or two hairlike tails, called flagella, make the colony move.

The cycle of life
Tiny one-celled animals called rotifers (below) eat Volvox, and baby fish eat rotifers. Bigger fish, tadpoles and birds all eat baby fish – and so the Sun's energy moves along a chain of living things.

ZOOM
x80

Green algae (they contain chlorophyll)

FACTOID

Seaweeds are algae. They are used to make medicines and foods, such as ice cream.

VITAL STATISTICS

Common name	Red algae
Latin name	*Antithamnion plumula*
Size	Up to 5 cm in length
Habitat	Rocky shores
Special feature	Each strand is one cell thick

Small but mighty
Diatoms look like nothing else on Earth. They are tiny algae that use a tough substance called silica to make their cell walls extra strong. Most diatoms live in seas and oceans.

TOWERS AND TUBES

Plants have important jobs to do. They position themselves to grab as much sunshine as possible, so they can photosynthesize and grow. They collect water from the soil, make food and move **nutrients** around. When you zoom inside a plant you can see exactly how it is able to carry out these essential tasks.

ACTUAL SIZE

Super highways

Stems work like strong but bendy towers, raising the leaves away from the soil so they can reach more light. They connect the food production areas – the leaves – with the plant's roots, flowers and fruits. Nutrients, such as minerals, food and water, travel along them.

ZOOM
x800

WHAT
IS IT?

Inside stems

Long tubes run the length of the stems. Some tubes carry water from the roots to the plant. They are called xylem vessels. Others carry food, mostly in the form of sugar, around the plant. They are called phloem tubes (say: flo-em).

ZOOM x90

Bendy bamboo

Air spaces between the cells keep the stem strong, but light and flexible. Bamboo stems have large hollow centres, and some types can grow up to 30 metres in height.

ZOOM x80

Staying strong

Simple plant cells are packed together like boxes. Each cell has **cellulose** in its walls, to make the plant strong. The dark area in a cell is the nucleus – it is the plant's control centre.

ZOOM x260

MOSS MOUNTAINS

Some of our planet's most amazing plants are ones we walk on, or over, without even noticing them. Mosses, for example, look just like bouncy, green cushions – until you zoom in on them. They can grow several metres wide, or may be so small that they can be seen only with a microscope.

Spore capsules fire spores into the air.

The leaves collect water.

FACTOID

Mosses have been around for about 300 million years, and there are more than 12,000 species, or types.

VITAL STATISTICS

Common name	Marsh moss
Latin name	*Sphagnum*
Size	10–40 mm in height
Habitat	Wet places
Special feature	Can hold lots of water in its structure

It is...

a water bear or moss piglet, and it hides in moss. It looks fearsome, but it's tiny: this image is magnified 220 times. If it dries out, a water bear can survive for ten years, 'frozen' in time until it gets wet again.

Lighter than air

Tiny moss **spores** have a tough outer coat to protect them. They are so small and light that they can float away on the lightest breeze.

ZOOM
x1000

ZOOM
x2

Moss

Exploding plants

The first plants that grew on land had no flowers or **seeds**. Today's mosses, **liverworts** and **ferns** are related to those early plants, and they also produce spores instead of seeds. Zoom into this moss and you can see tall stalks, called sporophytes. Each capsule at the top of a sporophyte holds thousands of spores.

ZOOM
x10

TALENTED TREES

Conifers are record-breaking plants. They are the tallest, smallest and oldest trees. Bonsai cypress trees and shore pines reach only 20 centimetres in height. Redwoods, by contrast, can reach heights of 95 metres, and one tree weighs ten times more than a blue whale. Amazingly, they grow from tiny seeds just 3 to 4 millimetres across.

◄ Dwarf conifers may grow just 3 centimetres a year, and never grow taller than one metre.

Extreme survivors

Many conifers can thrive in extreme habitats. Freezing winds and snow suit conifers in the far north, while those in dry places can endure months with no rain. Some Californian bristlecone pines have survived for 5000 years – and were hundreds of years old when the ancient Egyptians built the pyramids.

ACTUAL SIZE

ZOOM x6

WHAT IS IT?

Saving water

Conifer leaves are usually shaped like needles or scales, and coated with a waxy layer. This helps them to save water and survive in cold weather. Most conifers are evergreen, which means they don't lose their leaves every year.

Magic numbers

Pinecone scales are arranged in two sets of spirals – one anti-clockwise, and one clockwise. The number of spirals follows a unique mathematical sequence of numbers, called the **Fibonacci series**. It is the best way to pack in lots of scales, evenly and without gaps.

ACTUAL SIZE

ZOOM x3

Cones and seeds

One conifer tree grows both male and female cones. The yellow **pollen** on these little male cones will be carried, by wind, to the bigger female cones. The pollen **fertilizes** their eggs, but it takes up to three years for a female cone to mature. Once the seeds are grown, they fall to the ground.

ZOOM x2

FLOWERS IN FANCY DRESS

Trek through a rainforest and you will be surrounded by green. Huge emerald leaves, dangling green **creepers** and frilly fern **fronds** fill every space. Then your eye will catch the dazzling display of flowers, nestled in the crook of a tree. Showy, colourful and scented – flowers put on a bold display for a reason.

Orchid ZOOM x2

Big flower or little flowers?
*How big is a sunflower flower? You might think it is as big as your hand, or even bigger. Zoom in, and you will see that one sunflower head actually contains hundreds of flowers, each called a **floret** and no larger than your fingernail. Each floret produces one seed.*

ACTUAL SIZE

One petal, shaped like a landing platform, leads the insect towards the **nectary**.

It is...

a bee orchid. These flowers look and smell like female bees. When male bees try to mate with the flower, pollen rubs off on their back, which they accidentally transfer to other flowers.

Sugary liquid is produced in the nectary to attract insects.

Bright, colourful petals attract insects.

Pollen is carried on stamens. It brushes onto insects that pass by.

The **stigma** is connected to the ovary, which contains a flower's eggs.

FACTOID

The world's largest flowers are Rafflesias, and they stink of rotting meat. One flower can measure 90 centimetres wide.

VITAL STATISTICS

Common name	Rafflesia or corpse flower
Latin name	*Rafflesia arnoldii*
Size	90 cm across
Habitat	Rainforest
Special feature	Huge leathery petals

ZOOM x3

Secrets inside

*Scientists zoom into a plant's insides to understand how it reproduces. This flower has been cut in half, lengthways, to reveal its hidden reproductive organs. Long pollen-tipped **stamens** surround the carpel, which protects the tiny, round eggs that are nestling inside its fleshy tissues.*

PLANTS ON THE MOVE

When animals want to mate, it's easy. They can walk, swim or fly to find the perfect partner. Plants, however, are usually rooted to the ground. They overcome this problem by sending tiny parts of themselves – pollen – out into the world.

ZOOM x5

◀ Tiny granules of orange pollen coat the **anthers** of a lily flower. The anthers are the top part of a stamen.

What is pollen?

*Pollen contains male sex cells, which combine with female sex cells, or eggs, to make seeds. When pollen lands on a stigma – the female part of a flower – **pollination** has taken place. The pollen grows a tube down the stigma to reach the ovary, and then combines with an egg inside. This is called fertilization.*

Tough travellers

Some pollen grains are ribbed, or spiked; others are round, oval, flat or plump. It all depends on which plant they come from. The outer rind of a pollen grain is so tough it can survive for tens of thousands of years. One flower may produce thousands of pollen grains.

ZOOM x1000

Perfect pollinators

Pollen grains are small, which means they can travel easily – often on the wind. Many flowering plants rely on insects, such as this chafer beetle, for pollination. As they feed on plants the bugs get covered in pollen, which then rubs off onto stigmas.

ZOOM x6

Super small

Zoom into this flower anther to see little green grains of pollen. The smallest pollen grains are just 20 nanometres wide. One nanometre is a millionth of a millimetre!

ZOOM x70

ZOOM x5

WHAt iS it?

SEED JOURNEYS

Plants do not make caring parents. Once they have produced their seeds, most plants want their offspring to go as far away as possible! They don't want to be fighting for space, light and water. So they produce seeds that are well equipped to go on a long journey – by one means or another!

The pappus lifts the seed up in wind.

Each seed is attached so lightly to the plant that the smallest breeze will lift it up.

FACTOID

According to folklore, the number of puffs it takes to blow all the seeds off a dandelion seedhead tells you the time of day. Four puffs means it is four o'clock in the afternoon.

VITAL STATISTICS

Common name	Dandelion
Latin name	*Taraxacum officinale*
Size	5 to 20 cm in height
Habitat	Grassland and wasteland
Special feature	Each flowerhead can have more than 150 florets

ZOOM x2.5

Juicy fruits

After fertilization, some ovaries grow into fruits, or berries. Animals eat the fruits, and the seeds inside pass through their body, coming out in their faeces (say: fee-sees). In the right conditions, the seeds will germinate and grow into new plants.

Dandelion

ZOOM x3

New beginnings
*When a seed has the right conditions of water, soil and temperature, it may begin to grow a root, and eventually develop into a new plant. This is called **germination**.*

ZOOM x6

The fine hairs are called the pappus.

It is...
a burdock flower. Seeds develop inside the tough capsules, or burrs. Little hooks on a burr attach it to a passing animal, or person, and it is carried to a new place where the seeds may have the right conditions to grow.

GREEN DEFENDERS

Many animals, including us, know that plants can make tasty, healthy food. To survive, plants have some clever ways of defending themselves. Red yew berries look tasty, but are poisonous to some animals, and hard nuts are impossible for all but the strongest beaks to break.

Prickly plant
The peculiar shape of a cactus helps this prickly plant cope in a challenging environment. Sharp spines cover large green pads that look like giant leaves. In fact, the spines are leaves, and the pads are swollen stems. The stems store water – essential in a dry habitat where it rarely rains.

Sharp and cutting
Spines, spikes, prickles and thorns are a first line of defence for many plants. It would take a brave animal to place its jaws around a hairy mary plant. Each stem is smothered in needle-pointed spines, measuring up to 8 centimetres in length.

ACTUAL SIZE

Transferring poison

Milkweed produces toxic (poisonous) juice, or sap, which is deadly to most insects. Monarch caterpillars, however, eat the plant and store the deadly chemicals in their own body, making them poisonous to the animals that feed on them.

ZOOM x3

Toxic ooze

Storing poisonous chemicals in their tissues is another crafty way to deter hungry creatures. Rubber trees make sticky latex. It is toxic, but also traps insects trying to feed on the tree.

Plant attack

Hairs on a nettle leaf are tipped with tiny beads of **silica** (left). If you brush against the leaf, the tips will snap off and the hairs will spear your skin, injecting foul chemicals. One chemical causes pain, while another makes the skin swollen, red and itchy. Even grasses contain sharp pieces of silica.

ZOOM x100

WHAT IS IT?

ZOOM x4

MEAT-EATING PLANTS

When you look closely at plants, you begin to discover that they hold some strange, but deadly secrets.

In the endless battle for survival, animals usually turn plants into food – but in some rare cases, plants are the winners because they actually eat animals!

Red colour and sweet-smelling nectar attract insects.

FACTOID

Small flies can escape from the traps. This means the plant only spends time and energy on digesting larger meaty meals.

VITAL STATISTICS

Common name	Venus flytrap
Latin name	*Dionaea muscipula*
Size	Leaves are 5 to 30 cm in length
Habitat	Damp, mossy places
Special feature	The traps are closed for up to ten days, while a bug is digested

ZOOM x2

Extreme measures
The leaves of pitcher plants form colourful cups to attract insects. Curious bugs fall into the cups, which contain a potion of water and flesh-dissolving chemicals.

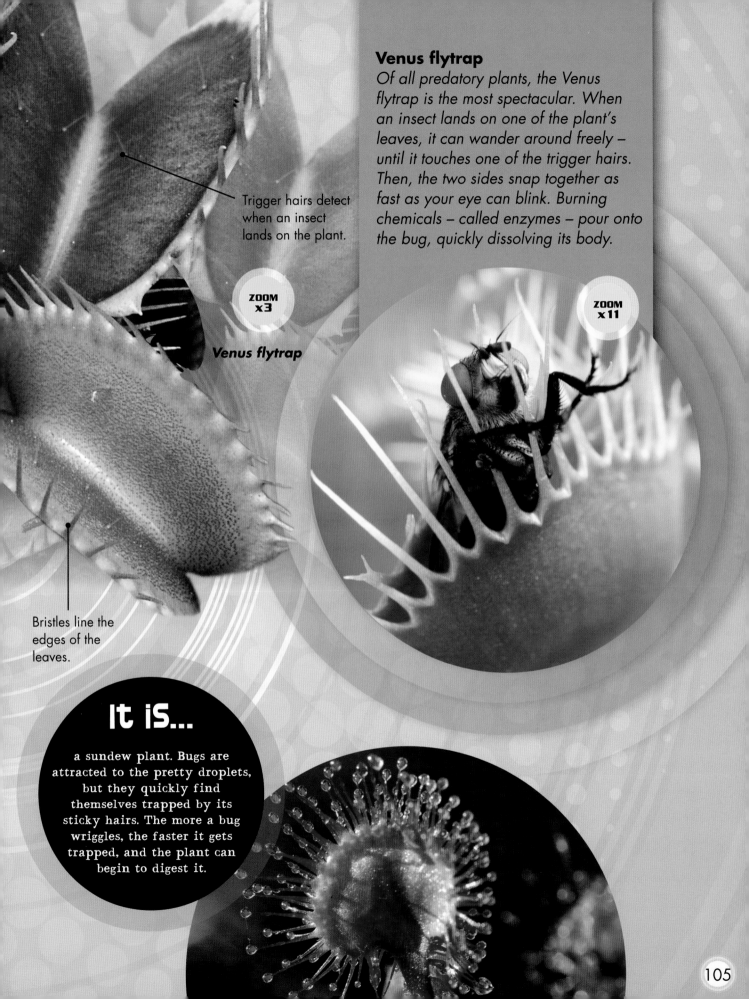

Venus flytrap

Of all predatory plants, the Venus flytrap is the most spectacular. When an insect lands on one of the plant's leaves, it can wander around freely – until it touches one of the trigger hairs. Then, the two sides snap together as fast as your eye can blink. Burning chemicals – called enzymes – pour onto the bug, quickly dissolving its body.

Trigger hairs detect when an insect lands on the plant.

ZOOM x3

Venus flytrap

ZOOM x11

Bristles line the edges of the leaves.

It is...

a sundew plant. Bugs are attracted to the pretty droplets, but they quickly find themselves trapped by its sticky hairs. The more a bug wriggles, the faster it gets trapped, and the plant can begin to digest it.

PLANT PARTNERS

Animals and plants depend on each other. Most animals eat plants, but many plants get something out of the relationship, too. Peer closely into the complex world of nature, and you will find out how living things often live in a strange kind of harmony.

Favouring fruit

Fruit bats do trees two big favours. When they feed on pollen, bats accidentally pollinate the flowers – which causes fruits to grow. They also disperse the tree's seeds by eating the fruits. The seeds pass through their body, and emerge in faeces, ready to grow into new plants.

WHAT IS IT?

ZOOM x8

Tough nuts

Agoutis are the only animals that are able to open the tough outer husk of a brazil nut. They have extremely strong incisor teeth, which keep growing throughout their lives. Brazil nut trees rely on agoutis to spread their seeds and if these rodents, which are endangered, died out, so would the trees.

Civet coffee

Palm civets enjoy the taste of juicy berries that grow on coffee plants. The seeds are partly digested, passed out in faeces and may germinate. In a strange twist, the seeds – coffee beans – are collected by people to be ground up and used to brew a delicious type of coffee – the most expensive in the world.

ZOOM x10

Taking in lodgers

*Acacia trees love having ants to stay. Ants not only attack insect pests, they even destroy nearby plants that might take light or water from the acacia.
In return, the tree rewards its ants by making little orange beads of food on their leaves. Ants feed the beads to their larvae (young).*

FRUITING FUNGI

When is a plant not a plant? When it is a fungus. These strange living things lead a very different life to green plants. Instead of using light to make food, fungi feed on living things or the remains of dead things. Mushrooms, **mould** and yeast are different types of fungus.

Fly agaric

ZOOM x2

Going underground

Fungi don't have roots. They have tiny feeding threads, called hyphae (say: hi-fee), which grow through soil, or the animal or plant they are feeding on. The hyphae absorb nutrients and can spread into dense networks that cover huge distances underground, making them the biggest living things on Earth.

It is...

a lichen. Scientists once thought lichens were types of plant, until they zoomed in close and discovered that a lichen is actually made up of a fungus and an alga living together.

The cap protects the gills, where spores are produced.

The fruiting body usually grows upwards, so the spores can disperse.

Fly agaric is the white-spotted red toadstool that is often illustrated in fairytales and other picture books.

VITAL STATISTICS

Common name	Fly agaric
Latin name	*Amanita muscaria*
Size	8–10 cm in length
Habitat	Under birch and spruce trees
Special feature	Poisonous and should NEVER be tasted

ZOOM x3000

Heads in the air

The part of a fungus we can usually spot, such as a mushroom, is called the fruiting body. It makes millions of microscopic spores that drift in the air. Bracket fungi grow huge fruiting spores on trees and rotting wood. The tiniest fruiting bodies are often moulds, and are microscopic in size.

USE YOUR EYES

Use your eyes to study these zooms that appear throughout the Plants section of this book. Can you recognize any of them just by looking at them? Are there any clues, such as colour or shape, that help you work out where you've seen these images before?

1 *I am a super-strong alga with silica to toughen me up.*

2 *Isn't nature brilliant? Look how neatly I am packed together, but what am I?*

3 *We may be tiny, but we are tough and can survive long journeys. We often travel by insect!*

4 *Ouch, these prickly spines have an important job to do.*

5 *Come close, we are snappy to see you!*

6 Small and tasty, we appeal to ants. What are we?

7 Huge needle-like spines cover my stems. I look scary!

8 I may be pretty but I hide a deep, dark secret. Do you know what I am?

9 Cut me in half, take a super-thin slice and put me under a microscope.

10 Gently blow and use me to tell the time.

11 My good looks appeal to people, but I want to impress those beautiful bees.

GLOSSARY

Algae Simple plants that photosynthesize, but do not have true stems and roots. Algae do not grow flowers. Seaweeds are algae.

Antennae Long, slender organs on an animal's head that help it to sense what is going on around it. They can usually detect touch, smell and taste.

Anther Part of a stamen that holds the pollen.

Barb A hair-like thread that grows from a feather's main shaft.

Barbule A tiny thread that grows from a barb.

Brood All of the eggs, or young, that are produced at one time.

Camouflage Colours or patterns that help an animal to stay hidden from view.

Cell Living things are made up of cells, which are often described as the building blocks of organisms.

Cellulose A tough substance that lines the walls of plant cells, giving them strength and structure.

Cocoon The silken case spun by an insect to protect the pupa.

Colony A group of animals that live closely together.

Creeper A plant that grows around another plant.

Crest Many birds have decorative feathers on their head, which are known as crests. They may be used to impress mates.

Crustacean An animal with four or more pairs of limbs, a body that is divided into segments and a tough exoskeleton. Most crustaceans live in water.

Cuticle The tough outer skin of a bug.

Digestive juice When an animal digests food, it breaks it down into smaller parts that can be absorbed into its body. Its body makes powerful liquids, called digestive juices or enzymes, to do this.

Downy Soft, fine and fluffy. Downy feathers are ideal for keeping a bird warm.

Echinoderm A type of marine animal that is often circular in shape and has a symmetry of five. Sea urchins, starfish and brittle stars are echinoderms.

Eye-spot Some animals have patterns on their body that resemble the eyes of larger animals. These eye-spots may help to scare away predators.

Fern A plant with feathery fronds. They do not have flowers, and they produce spores rather than seeds.

Fertilize When a male sex cell joins with a female sex cell. After fertilization in plants, a seed may grow.

Fibonacci series A number series in which each number is the sum of the two numbers before it, e.g. 1, 1, 2, 3, 5, 8 etc.

Floret A small flower that is one of many that make up a flowerhead.

Food chain A chain of animals that depend on each other for food. Plants are normally at the bottom of a food chain; they are eaten by one animal, which is eaten by another animal, and so on.

Frond A leaf-like part of a fern.

Fry Baby fish. When they first hatch they are sometimes called larvae.

Gene Animal cells contain genes, which hold all of the information necessary for the animal to live, grow and reproduce.

Germination When a seed begins to grow.

Gills Organs that are used to take oxygen out of water, and to pass the waste gas (carbon dioxide) out of the body. Fish have gills.

Global warming The warming of the Earth's atmosphere. This means the oceans are also getting hotter.

Grub Young, soft-bodied bugs are larvae, but they are also sometimes called grubs or maggots.

Invertebrate An animal that does not have a backbone. Molluscs, worms and insects are invertebrates.

Iridescence Colours that seem to change when they are seen from different angles are described as iridescent.

Katydid A green or brown insect that belongs to the same family as crickets and grasshoppers.

Keratin A tough substance that is used in nature to make skin, nails, hair, scales, hooves and feathers.

Larva (plural: larvae) A young, soft-bodied bug. It will eventually change and grow into an adult.

Lens A transparent object with curved sides that gathers light and bends light rays. Lenses in eyes focus light rays into the back of the eye, so an animal can see. Lenses in cameras and microscopes are made of glass and can magnify an image.

Life cycle The way an animal begins its life, grows, reproduces and eventually dies.

Liverwort A simple plant with leaves that have lobes. Liverworts live in moist places and do not grow flowers.

Macro lens Used in a camera to take photographs close to the subject, such as a bug.

Mandible The mouthparts of a bug.

Mantid This insect is also known as a mantis, and is related to the cockroach.

Membrane A thin layer, like a sheet, that separates the inside parts of an animal's body or makes a lining around organs.

Metamorphosis The way that a young bug, or larva, changes into an adult.

Mollusc An invertebrate with a soft body that usually lives in damp places or water habitats, such as the ocean. Snails, octopuses, shellfish and squid are molluscs. Most molluscs grow shells.

Mould Fungi that are commonly found growing on food or decaying matter. They are very small organisms, but can grow into large colonies and cause disease.

Moult When a bug grows bigger and sheds its old skin, or cuticle.

Nectary Part of a flower that produces a sweet liquid called nectar. Nectar attracts insects to the plant.

Nutrient A substance that helps an organism to live and grow.

Organ An area of the body, such as the brain, lung or heart, that performs a special job.

Oxygen The gas that is produced by plants, and that animals breathe to live.

Parasite A living thing that survives by feeding from, or living in, another animal or plant, known as a 'host'. Parasites always harm the host.

Photophore An organ that produces light.

Photosynthesis The process by which plants use the Sun's light to make food.

Pigment Chemicals that give an animal colour.

Plume This is another word for a feather, especially one that is colourful or downy.

Pollen The yellow dust on a flower's stamens. Each pollen grain contains a single male sex cell. If it combines with a plant's egg, the egg is fertilized, and a seed can grow.

Pollination When pollen is transferred to the female part of a flower.

Proboscis A long, slender mouthpart through which some bugs absorb liquid.

Protein Essential substances that all living things need to grow, because cells are made of protein.

Pupa The stage of an insect's life cycle when it is going through the change from larva to adult. It is in a tough case, called a chrysalis, which protects it at this time.

Rachis The central shaft of a feather.

Scavenge A method of feeding that involves finding and eating any available food, including animals that have died naturally.

Seed A plant's unit of reproduction. It can, in the right circumstances, grow into another plant.

Silica A tough mineral that occurs naturally in some plants.

Spiderling A young spider that has just hatched from its egg.

Spore The unit of reproduction for some simple plants, and fungi. Spores can, under the right circumstances, grow into plants.

Stamen The male part of a flower. It has two parts: a filament that is topped by a pollen-coated anther.

Stigma The female part of a flower that receives the pollen during pollination.

Talons A bird of prey's powerful, clawed feet.

Tropical The 'tropics' are a region of the Earth near the Equator, between the Tropic of Cancer and the Tropic of Capricorn. Tropical areas have days and nights of similar length, and have hot climates.

Ultraviolet A type of light that cannot be seen by humans, but is visible to many other animals – especially insects.

Venom A type of poison that is made by animals and injected into another animal's body, often by biting or stinging.

Wingspan The measurement across both of a bird's outstretched wings. The measurement is taken from tip to tip.

INDEX

acacia trees 107

algae 88–89, 108, 112

anemones 66–67, 71

antennae 19

ants 18–19

assassin bugs 17

bamboo 91

bee-eaters 47

bees 26–27

beetles 13, 24, 25

bills 37, 41, 44, 46–47, 48, 56

birds of prey 47, 54

bites 18, 19, 27, 30, 31

blowflies 12

blue whale 62

bones 39

bowerbirds 53

brains 14, 18

burdock 101

butterflies 22–23

cactus 102

camouflage 10, 11, 20–21, 37, 42

caterpillars 21, 23

cells 88, 91, 98, 109, 112

cellulose 91, 112

centipedes 17

chickens 50, 51

chicks 44, 50–51, 52, 53, 57

chlorophyll 89

clams 74

claws 15, 16–17, 18, 24, 25

clownfish 67

cocoons 13, 23

colonies 18, 19, 27, 48, 50

colours 22–23, 28–29

comb jellies 83

cone shells 73

conifers 94–95

coots 55

coral 71, 76–77, 78, 79

crabs 67, 75, 77, 78–79

cranes 42

crests 42

crustaceans 70, 112

currents 79

cuticle 12, 13

dandelions 100–101

deepwater animals 80–83

diatoms 89

digestive juices 16, 17

downy feathers 37, 43

dragonflies 14–15

ducks 55

eagles 38, 47, 54

echinoderms 64, 65, 113

eggs 19, 27, 40, 50–51, 53, 56, 65, 69, 75, 78, 83

energy 88, 89

eyes 10, 14, 18, 19, 30

eyesight 36, 45

eye-spots 22

feathers 36, 37, 41, 42–43, 44, 49, 50

ferns 93, 113

fertilization 95, 98, 100, 113

Fibonacci series 95, 113

finches 44–45, 47

fish 67, 68–71, 81, 82–83

flapping 39

fleas 25

fledglings 51

flight 14, 15, 26, 37, 38–39, 40, 43

florets 96, 113

flowers 96–97, 101

food chains 62, 113

fossils 63

fruits 100, 102, 104

fry 69, 113

fungi 108–109

genes 29
germination 100, 101, 81, 113
gills 69, 113
glasseye snappers 69
global warming 77, 113
goose barnacles 65
Great Barrier Reef 77
grubs *see larvae*
guillemots 56

hatchet fish 81
hovering 40
hummingbirds 40–41
hydrothermal vents 81

incubation 51
insulation 43
invertebrates 72, 113
iridescence 41

jaws 15, 16–17, 18, 24, 25
jellyfish 79, 80
jumping 25

katydids 20
keratin 42
kingfishers 39
krill 62–63

larvae 12, 13, 15, 18, 23,
    27, 78, 79, 80, 114
leaf insects 11
lenses 8, 14
lichens 82
life cycles 12–13
lionfish 70–71
liverworts 93, 114
locusts 17

macaws 48
mackerel 70
macro photography 6–7
maggots *see larvae*
mandibles 17, 18, 25
mantids 10–11, 34
mating 45, 51
meat-eating plants
    104–105
metamorphosis 12, 23
microscopes 4, 6–7
milkweed 103
mimicry 48
mimics 11
molluscs 72, 74,
114

mosses 92–93
moths 13, 23
moulds 108, 109, 114
moulting 12, 13
mynahs 48

nectary 96, 97, 114
nests 40, 52–53
nettles 103
nutrients 90, 108, 114
nuts 107
nymphs 15

obelias 63
octopuses 74–75, 83
ostriches 55
ovaries 97
owls 36–37
oxygen 69, 88, 115

parasites 44

parrots 48–49

passerines 55

pellets 37

penguins 43, 53, 55

phloem tubes 91

photophores 26, 115

photosynthesis 88, 90, 114

pigments 22, 29, 34

pincers 15, 16–17, 18, 24, 25

pinecones 95

pitcher plants 104

plankton 4, 62–63, 65, 29, 81

plumage *see feathers*

pollen and pollination 24, 26,
    95, 96, 97, 98–99,
    106, 114

polyps 76, 77, 78, 78

proboscis 23

puffins 56–57

pupae 12, 18, 34

queens 18, 19, 27

radiolarians 63

Rafflesias 97

reefs 69, 76–77, 78

remotely operated vehicles
    (ROVs) 80

rock pools 64

rotifers 89

rubber trees 103

scavengers 47, 54, 78

sea horses 65

sea slugs and snails 72, 73

sea urchins 65

seaweeds 89

seeds 95, 96, 98, 100–101,
    106, 107, 114

sessile animals 67

sharks 68, 71

shrimps 70, 71, 75

silica 89, 103, 114

snails 29

social insects 19

spiders 16, 21, 24, 28, 30–31

spines 65, 70, 74, 102

spores 92, 93, 109, 114

squid 72, 80

stamens 97, 98, 114

starfish 64, 76

stems 90–91

stigmas 97, 98, 99, 114

stings 18, 19, 27, 30, 31,
    66, 79

stonefish 74

sundew plants 79

swimming 25, 55, 56

talons 54, 60

tarantulas 30–31

toucans 46

toxic juices 77, 78, 79

treehoppers 21

trout 69

ultraviolet light 14, 22

venom 17, 30, 31, 65, 66,
    71, 73, 74, 75

Venus flytraps 104–105

viperfish 82–83

Volvox 88–89

water 90, 95, 102

water bears 92

waterbirds 55

water boatmen 25

weavers 52

webbed feet 55, 56

wings 15, 19, 22

wingspan 37, 41

worms 28

xylem vessels 91

yeast 108, 109

NOTES FOR PARENTS AND TEACHERS

How do lenses work?

Photography and microscopy are two ways in which the physics of light and lenses can be applied to our everyday lives. Find some books in your local library or use the Internet* to track down diagrams that show how lenses bend (refract) light passing through them. Look at diagrams that show both convex and concave lenses, to discover how the shape of a lens changes the effect. Together, you can work out which of these two types of lens is used in microscopes, telescopes and binoculars.

You can also use the Internet to explore the role of lenses in the human eye, and how corrective lenses in spectacles are used to improve eyesight.

Make your own water lens

It is easy to make a water lens that shows how even a simple lens can magnify images. Lay a piece of clingfilm or other transparent plastic over a piece of newspaper text. Place a single drop of water on the plastic. You will notice that the text beneath the water drop is magnified. Find out what happens when you make the drop bigger, or smaller.

Finding crawly creatures

Take a walk to the park with some plastic containers, a magnifying glass, a sketch book, a ruler and some pencils. See how many bugs you can collect in your containers.

Look at them closely with the magnifying glass and make a list of them all. If you don't know the name of an insect, make a drawing of it or take its picture with a mobile phone, and use a book or the Internet to identify it once you get home. Which ones have spots and which ones have wings? How many legs do they have? Do any have pincers? Which ones might be camouflaged? When looking at bugs make sure to be gentle so you don't harm them, and always put them back where you found them.

*The publishers cannot accept any liability for the content of Internet websites, including third-party websites.

Mini birdwatchers

Take a walk outdoors and listen for birdsong. Count how many different types of bird you can hear. Can you imitate the songs you hear? When you see a bird you can make a note of identifiers, such as size, colour, tail length and beak shape. While you are walking keep an eye out for any feathers on the ground. Bring them home and use them as the start of a bird spotting scrapbook. Also keep an ear out for the sound of baby birds in their nests. Why do you think they might be making such a racket?

You can also zoom further into the world of birds with a pair of binoculars and an identification book. This simple activity helps children learn the rewards of sitting quietly and observing.

Seaside activities

Rockpools are a magnificent place to get a glimpse of what lives in our oceans and seas. Take a trip to the seaside and try to find a small rockpool to observe. Collect stones, shells and pieces of seaweed, and look at them closely.

Once you have established that water bends light, encourage the child to experiment with the way an image can appear distorted when seen through water. Do the colours on a shell appear brighter or more muted when they are underwater?

Discuss who might live in the shells and why they might be empty. Has a predator eaten what is inside? If you find any shells with animals still living in them, leave them where you found them – if there's an animal inside, it is somebody's home!

Plant life for youngsters

Help children to explore the ways we all use plants. Discuss how wheat seeds and yeast are used to make bread. Find out how cotton grows, and is turned into fabric. Point out that many everyday items, such as pencils, paper and bedsheets, are made from plant materials. Search your local park for any leaves, seeds and nuts on the ground and take them home if you don't think any animals will mind. Discuss the difference between a nut, a seed, a flower and a leaf. Leaves can be traced around and the tracings can then be coloured in.

You can also take paper and pencils to a forest and make rubbings of the different tree barks. What is the purpose of bark and how does it protect trees?

Respecting nature

Teach children to respect the wildlife around them. They can watch wildlife, visit the seaside and observe the world around them without harming it.

Encourage them to understand that plants are often animals' habitats and food sources, and that animals and their homes must not be disturbed. When out walking make sure you set a good example by leaving the environment clean and pick up any rubbish you might come across.

Taking care of the environment — and yourself!

Discussing ways of protecting the environment is a good way to encourage children to appreciate the natural world. Also remind children that some plants, such as stinging nettles, can sting or are poisonous, and some have thorns, so they should exercise care when out exploring.

Early beginnings

Many naturalists discover a love of wildlife simply by observing animals, sketching or photographing them, and making notes about their behaviour.